Badiou Reframed

Contemporary Thinkers Reframed Series

Adorno Reframed ISBN: 978 1 84885 947 0
Geoff Boucher

Badiou Reframed ISBN: 978 1 78076 260 9
Alex Ling

Bakhtin Reframed ISBN: 978 1 78076 512 9
Deborah Haynes

Baudrillard Reframed ISBN: 978 1 84511 678 1
Kim Toffoletti

Deleuze Reframed ISBN: 978 1 84511 547 0
Damian Sutton & David Martin-Jones

Derrida Reframed ISBN: 978 1 84511 546 3
K. Malcolm Richards

Guattari Reframed ISBN: 978 1 78076 233 3
Paul Elliott

Heidegger Reframed ISBN: 978 1 84511 679 8
Barbara Bolt

Kristeva Reframed ISBN: 978 1 84511 660 6
Estelle Barrett

Lacan Reframed ISBN: 978 1 84511 548 7
Steven Z. Levine

Lyotard Reframed ISBN: 978 1 84511 680 4
Graham Jones

Merleau-Ponty Reframed ISBN: 978 1 84885 799 5
Andrew Fisher

Badiou Reframed

Interpreting Key Thinkers for the Arts

Alex Ling

I.B. TAURIS

Published in 2017 by
I.B.Tauris & Co. Ltd
London • New York
www.ibtauris.com

Copyright © 2017 Alex Ling

The right of Alex Ling to be identified as the author of this work
has been asserted by him in accordance with the Copyright,
Designs and Patents Act 1988.

All rights reserved. Except for brief quotations in a review, this book,
or any part thereof, may not be reproduced, stored in or introduced
into a retrieval system, or transmitted, in any form or by any means,
electronic, mechanical, photocopying, recording or otherwise, without the
prior written permission of the publisher.

ISBN: 978 1 78076 260 9
eISBN: 978 1 78672 062 7
ePDF: 978 1 78673 062 6

A full CIP record for this book is available from the British Library
A full CIP record for this book is available from the Library
of Congress

Library of Congress catalog card: available

Typeset in Egyptienne F by Riverside Publishing Solutions, Salisbury
Page design by Chris Bromley
Printed and bound by CPI Group (UK) Ltd, Croydon, CR0 4YY

Contents

List of illustrations vii

Introduction. First impressions 1

PART ONE: BEING AND APPEARING

Chapter 1. Unframing, enframing, reframing 21

Chapter 2. Philosophy under condition 43

PART TWO: EVENT AND SUBJECT

Chapter 3. The shock of the new 67

Chapter 4. The subject of art 87

PART THREE: TRUTH AND ETHICS

Chapter 5. From here to eternity 113

Chapter 6. Keeping the faith 135

Conclusion. Badiou reframed 155

Notes 159

Bibliography 170

Index 175

looking from black —
" " white —

[dark field] — scattered light, or
emitted light is source
of contrast
self-illumination
oblique illumination   fluorescence

[bright field] — absorbed light
is source of
[the stain]   contrast.

the depths .

tracers —

List of illustrations

Figure 1. Still from *The Wizard of Oz*, Victor Fleming, 1939, Metro-Goldwyn-Mayer. 15

Figure 2. Kasimir Malevich, *White on White*, 1918, Museum of Modern Art, New York, Photo credit: SCALA/Art Resource, NY. 30

Figure 3. Mark Rothko, *Ochre and Red on Red*, 1954, Phillips Collection, Washington DC. 37

Figure 4. Still from *Suspicion*, Alfred Hitchcock, 1941, RKO Radio Pictures, Inc. 52

Figure 5. Still from *Film*, Alan Schneider, 1965, Milestone Film & Video, Inc. 59

Figure 6. Marcel Duchamp, *Fountain*, 1917, photo by Alfred Steiglitz in *The Blind Man* 2. 67

Figure 7. Detail from Stéphane Mallarmé, *A Throw of the Dice*, 1897, *Collected Poems* © University of California Press Books, 2011. 93

Figure 8. Alberto Giacometti, *Suspended Ball*, 1930–1 (1965 version), Alberto Giacometti Foundation © Fondation Alberto et Annette Giacometti/Licensed by Viscopy, 2016. 121

Figure 9. Pablo Picasso, *Violin and Grapes*, 1912, Museum of Modern Art, New York, Photo credit: SCALA/Art Resource, NY.   131

Figure 10. Banksy, *Untitled*, Segregation wall, Palestine, 2005.   137

Introduction

First impressions

Alain Badiou is without doubt one of the most important philosophers writing today. Perhaps only a handful of other living philosophers can be said to display as diverse a field of reference, as broad a range of influence, and as powerful an ability to intervene in contemporary debates. Still fewer can lay claim to establishing as meticulous and systematic a philosophy (let alone one that truly begins 'from scratch', constructing its edifice from the ground up, as it were).

Yet if Badiou is one of the most important contemporary philosophers, he is at the same time one of the most polarizing. This is at least in part a consequence of the extraordinary range and rigour of his undertaking. On the one hand, the breadth of his project alone is astounding, ranging as it does from the void of 'pure multiplicity' through the 'plenitude of appearance' up to the paradox of events and the subjects and truths they might engender (or again, from *nothing* up to *everything*, and then again beyond that). Yet on the other hand, the infinite wealth of his system is offset by equally stark austerity measures, Badiou unhesitatingly jettisoning everything he deems to be 'unimportant' (if not outright harmful) not only for philosophy itself but also for thinking more generally. Indeed, polemics to one side – and Badiou is certainly one of the great polemicists of our age – newcomers to his thought, in particular those with a background in the creative arts, will likely find his philosophy either infinitely expansive, opening up previously unimaginable possibilities, or uncomfortably, even debilitatingly, restrictive.

To be sure, a quick skim through one of his more immediately accessible works such as *Ethics: An Essay on the Understanding of Evil* or *Infinite Thought* is likely to reveal Badiou as either an emphatically modern, and in this sense, truly revolutionary thinker, or alternatively, an anachronistic dogmatist, depending on your vantage point. Conversely, a detailed reading of his magnum opus *Being and Event* – which remains to this day the central text of his philosophy, the work in which his system is most fully and systematically elaborated – should throw up a different but no less divisive situation, this time involving the acceptance or not of his initial declaration that 'mathematics is ontology'.[1] Either you agree with this bold thesis, making it difficult not to go along with the meticulously drawn-out consequences that constitute the remainder of this dense but incredibly rewarding tome, or you disagree, and Badiou's entire philosophy is accordingly unfounded. The aim of this short book is consequently not only to provide an overview of Badiou's philosophical system, with the visual arts as both our inspiration and our guide, but also to explain exactly how it is that his thought elicits such conflicting reactions, and why such polemicizing is moreover an integral – and indeed, *essential* – function of thought itself.

Before we begin, however, it is worth pointing out at least one immediate reason as to why Badiou's philosophy provokes such extreme reactions. This can be summarized in a single word: *mathematics*.

It is one of the great pedagogical ironies that mathematics, that most stable and universal of languages – the language that Plato, in his *Meno*, demonstrated could be equally comprehended by educated man and slave alike – frequently serves as the greatest bulwark against the successful communication of ideas. For the very second in which mathematical concepts arise in a text, a great many 'non-mathematically minded' readers (and I count myself among this number) will demonstrate an unfortunate tendency to 'tune out'. Due no doubt to its perceived complexity, it is mathematics' unenviable fate to be something that is, at one and the same time, inclusive *and* exclusive, embracing *and* alienating, transparent *and* impenetrable.

To say that mathematics is central to Badiou's philosophy would be a gross understatement. As such, one cannot approach his work with any degree of rigour without engaging with mathematics on some level. That said, this book has been written with the non-mathematically inclined reader foremost in mind, and every possible effort has been taken to keep the demonstrations as simple and clear as possible, detailing only those elements that are absolutely essential to a proper comprehension of Badiou's overall philosophy. More than this, the central conceit of the series to which this book belongs – namely, that of 'reframing' complex philosophical concepts and ideas through the visual arts – requires that the mathematical abstractions be 'propped up' not only philosophically, but moreover with concrete artistic supplements (hence Malevich's *White on White* accounts for the distinction between 'counted' and 'uncounted' multiplicity, while the paradoxical notion of a set's 'auto-belonging' is encapsulated in Duchamp's *Fountain*, etc).

Nonetheless, as Badiou declares, 'the philosopher can and must love this mathematical world where the concept is so pure and so strong that it renders intuition ridiculous',[2] and the reader is accordingly strongly encouraged to take the time to engage with Badiou's mathematical foundations – for they truly are, philosophically speaking, *foundational* – as in doing this they will find the experience infinitely richer, more comprehensible, and ultimately more rewarding.

One final point before we begin. The fact that this book turns to the visual arts in order to introduce and 'reframe' Badiou's work may appear to carry with it the assumption that philosophy enjoys a certain authority over the arts, or that the philosopher can 'educate' the artist about their own work. Now, Badiou certainly has much to say about the arts. One of his central tenets, after all, is that art is not an object for philosophy, but rather one of its fundamental *conditions*. That said, proclaiming art's 'conditional' status is in no way to suggest that art serves, or is somehow subordinate to, philosophy. To the contrary, the relationship is, if anything, the other way around. For while philosophy has a definite need for art, art can happily make do without philosophy. Or to put it another way, while philosophy can doubtless be extremely useful for art (particularly concerning key concepts like creation, subjectivity and truth – concepts that constitute the very core of this book), this does not make it *necessary*.

Philosophy, on the other hand, absolutely needs art. Indeed, without art, philosophy does not – *cannot* – exist. Exactly why this is the case is something that we will be exploring throughout this book. For now, it is simply worth keeping this asymmetrical relationship in mind, and being aware that even though artworks often (but not always) play an exegetic role here, the fact of the matter is that art – *real* art – always comes *before* philosophy, instructing it, as it were, on what it is, on what it can be, and on what it might become.

The materiality of the new

Born in Rabat, Morocco in 1937, and educated at the Lycée Louis-Le-Grand and the prestigious École Normale Supérieure, Badiou began his career as a high school teacher before taking up a position (under the direction of Michel Foucault) in 1969 at the newly established 'experimental' University of Paris VIII (Vincennes-Saint Denis). By this time Badiou had already published two novels, *Almagestes* and *Portulans*; written one book of philosophy, *Le Concept de modèle* (*The Concept of Model*); and had been deeply affected by the student and worker uprisings of May 1968. He remained at the University of Paris VIII for thirty years, during which time he published numerous important works of philosophy including his first major work *Théorie du sujet* (*Theory of the Subject*) and his undisputed magnum opus, *L'Être et l'événement* (*Being and Event*). In 1999 he returned to the École Normale Supérieure as head of the philosophy department.

Badiou continues to run a regular seminar at the Collège International de Philosophie while at the same time publishing a diverse array of works, ranging from bestselling polemics against French presidents (*De quoi Sarkozy est-il le nom?; The Meaning of Sarkozy*) to philosophical reappraisals of great composers (*Five Lessons on Wagner*), to books expounding complex mathematical concepts for schoolchildren (*Le fini et l'infini*). In 2006 he published his third 'major' work and belated 'sequel' to his earlier magnum opus, *Logiques des mondes: l'être et l'événement, 2* (*Logics of Worlds: Being and Event, 2*) and to this day he continues to ramify and extend his philosophical system. Among his many current projects – which include a film on *The Life of Plato* – a third volume of *Being and Event* elaborating further on the work of the subject is currently in the works, to be titled *L'immanence des vérités* (*The Immanence of Truths*). At last count he has published more than 40 works of philosophy, as well as numerous plays and novels, each of which in one way or another elaborate on and extend his overall philosophical project.

So what exactly is Badiou's project? At bottom, his work is nothing short of a rigorous attempt to think *novelty itself*; at one end a thinking of how something new – and, crucially, *universal* – arrives in a world, and at the other of how real global change can come about. In his own words:

my unique philosophical question, I would say, is the following: can we think that there is something new in the situation, not outside the situation nor the new somewhere else, but can we really think through novelty and treat it in the situation? The system of philosophical answers that I elaborate, whatever its complexity may be, is subordinated to that question and none other.[3]

Which is to say that the entirety of Badiou's vast conceptual apparatus, from the mathematical inscription of pure multiplicity, through the logical articulation of worlds, all the way up to extra-ontological events and the subjects and truths they can bring about – all of this is deployed in an elaborate attempt to think 'the materiality of the new'.[4]

Given this 'novel' focus, a good place for us to start would be to ask the obvious question: what is 'the new'? Or again, what in the world would constitute real novelty?

The first point to make here is that true innovation, so far as Badiou understands it, has nothing whatsoever to do with what we generally understand in terms of 'progress'. Positive or not, the innumerable developments that take place around us on a daily basis – from diplomatic or technological 'breakthroughs' up to the latest 'blockbuster' exhibition – for the most part merely form a branch of what one of Badiou's proclaimed 'masters', the French psychoanalyst Jacques Lacan, famously called the 'service of goods' (*service des biens*), namely, the circulation of knowledges and practices that ultimately work to reinforce the established order.

So while our information technology industries (to take a single and obvious example) are doubtless advancing at a breathtaking pace – so much so that it can seem almost impossible to keep up to speed with the latest technological developments – this does not necessarily mean that there is anything truly *new* at work in the situation. From a Badiouian perspective, regardless of how exciting such advances may be, their mode of production (which is not necessarily to say their method of employment) is in fact for the most part *monotonous*. For in the final analysis, what we bear witness to here are so many extensions, repetitions, recyclings and superficial transformations of forms of knowledge that are already operating in the situation, and which (and herein lies the rub) inevitably work to *reproduce the dominant order*. Simply put, far from representing (as one popular slogan puts it) 'change we can believe in', what such advancements paradoxically ensure is precisely that things *stay exactly the same*.

By contrast, real novelty – the kind that is both the focus of and the driving force behind Badiou's work (and, it hardly needs to be said, every true artistic creation) – is something that radically breaks with this kind of monotonous production. A single spark that ignites a political revolution, an amorous encounter that turns your life upside down, a new scientific theory compelling us to change our understanding of the world, a formal innovation which forces us to reassess the limitations as much as the possibilities of art: suddenly and unpredictably, something *happens* in the world and ruptures with its prevailing logic by pointing to a previously unimaginable *possibility*, something that had hitherto been impossible or unthinkable (as opposed to simply unconsidered).

This sudden 'interruption of repetition' is precisely what Badiou calls an *event*, and it is the pivot on which his entire philosophy – or what he has recently come to call his 'materialist dialectic' – turns.

This being said, we should take care not to reduce Badiou's thought to a mere 'philosophy of the event'. Indeed, placing to one side the theoretical *tours des force* that are Badiou's mathematical ontology and logical phenomenology (which we will be working through in Part One of this book), an event on its own is not nearly enough to bring about real and lasting change: while it certainly introduces something radically new or heretofore 'un-known' into the situation, an event is itself entirely incapable of sustaining this novelty. A revolution, we know, is quickly quashed without militant commitment, just as a brief encounter alone is not enough to sustain a lifetime of love.

To the contrary, and in spite of its momentous effects, an event is in fact as rare and fleeting as it is fragile. A puncture hole in the fabric of the world, an event, if left unattended to, is all-too quickly patched up by the forces that dominate and govern the situation, forces that Badiou terms the *state of the situation* (or simply the 'state'), and which effectively establish a 'static' regime of repetition. For in rupturing with the situation – whose laws, as we will shortly see, in fact serve to prohibit any form of newness – an event is a fundamentally *illegal* occurrence; it is, by definition, an enemy of the state. As such, its fate is to vanish as soon as it arises: as Badiou puts it in *Logics of Worlds*, an event (or more precisely, an event's material support, called its *site*) 'is an ontological figure of the instant: it appears only to disappear'.[5] To this end, if an event is to have any durable effect – if it is to bring about any real and lasting change in the world – it requires dedicated, disciplined, selfless – in a word, *militant* – support.

This post-eventual support takes the form of an affirmative or 'faithful' *subject*, which, in recognizing the event *as* an event – or more precisely, in declaring that it *was* an event (given that an event's fate is to vanish almost as soon as it appears) – sets about drawing forth the consequences of its having happened, namely, the new *possibilities* opened up by its sudden appearance (and equally sudden disappearance). Solicited by a vanished event, the subject constitutes itself around its lingering *trace* (for even though its fate is to immediately disappear, every event nonetheless leaves a mark of sorts, being the sudden possibility of what was previously impossible) and draws forth its manifold consequences.

It is to the subject's arduous and protracted working-out of these novel consequences (or the creative experimentation with the new possibilities implied by the event) that Badiou gives the name *truth-procedure*. If the event is the pivot on which Badiou's philosophy turns, the truth-procedure is the direction in which it swings.

The elephant in the room

Placing (momentarily) to one side the important question of what exactly Badiou means by 'truth', let us note in passing that, like the event itself, a truth-procedure – the single and sole path pursued by a faithful subject – designates something fundamentally *exceptional* (in every sense of the word). For one thing, it can only take place in the wake of a vanished event. This occurrence is furthermore restricted to four different 'generic procedures' or 'conditions' (so-called because they work to 'condition' philosophy), being *art*, *politics*, *science* and *love*. (As we will see, there is no such thing as a '*philosophical* truth-procedure'.) More than this, like the truth it constructs, a truth-procedure has as its material only those resources that are readily available in the situation.

Exactly how this comes to be is somewhat complicated, involving difficult meditations on the nature of truth, infinity and universality, and we will be spending a good deal of this book fleshing out the details. For the purposes of this introduction, however, we can get a basic idea of the process if we consider the difference between 'knowledge' and 'thought' *per se*.

As we saw in our earlier, rather hastily sketched example of the information technology industry, in spite of its pretentions toward fuzzy ideals like 'growth' and 'progress', the realm of knowledge is in actual fact a decidedly conservative and 'static' affair, inasmuch as it is essentially structured according to the interests of the state. As Badiou sees it, while we are constantly surrounded by (and contribute to) various knowledges, it is only on very rare occasions that we experience real *thought* in action. For unlike knowledge, any and every instance of real thinking is, by its very nature, a fundamentally *creative act* – an act of invention that necessarily breaks with the status quo – and is to this effect radically *subtracted* from both knowledge and the state. In a word, to think and to create – truly, radically, and absolutely – are one and the same thing. Or to put it somewhat aphoristically, thought is always the thought of the un-known.

Now, as we saw above, Badiou designates the 'state' the set of mechanisms that govern and dominate the situation. Ordinarily, the domination of the state over a situation is, for reasons we will examine shortly, both absolute and beyond determination. What a subjective truth-procedure (or 'thought' *per se*, for they are one and the same thing) does in effect – and this is where it gets a little complicated – is assign a precise measure to this otherwise indeterminate excess. That is to say, it figures out exactly how 'big' the state really is. At the same time however, the truth-procedure itself (again, for complicated reasons that we will explore shortly) remains 'subtracted' from all particularity, that is, from everything 'known' by the state, or from everything that falls into the realm of knowledge (what Badiou terms the 'encyclopaedia' of the situation). In this manner it is able to evade or 'distance' itself from statist domination. Or in other words, by recognizing the true reach of the state, the subject is able to keep it at arms-length while going about its core business of changing the world.

This in mind, the necessary and sufficient conditions of a subjective truth-procedure might be very summarily outlined in the following way.

First, an event – which for the present we can define as a momentary, localized and entirely unpredictable rupture in the order of things – suddenly adds to, and is then 'subtracted' from, a situation. That is to say, an event – aleatory, illegal, excessive – literally flashes in and out of existence.

However, insofar as the 'place' in which the event takes place – what Badiou calls the *site* – is, as we will see, precisely the 'voided' part of the situation, the place of radical 'inappearance' (that is, a point which for complex reasons remains altogether unrecognized by the state), there can accordingly be no *knowledge* of its occurrence for the simple reason that, in falling outside of the statist order, it is thereby subtracted from all predication.

Moreover, the event itself having since vanished, its *trace* – which is to say its immediate consequence (namely, the sudden and absolute appearance of what had previously 'inexisted', or what had heretofore been 'cancelled out' by the logic of the world in question) – is only sustained thereafter by means of a faithful subject that, having decided affirmatively in favour of the event's belonging to the situation (and establishing, if you can forgive the Rumsfeldian pun, a 'known unknown'), only comes into being by exerting a militant fidelity to the (unverifiable) fact that the event did indeed take place.

Following which, by way of an arduous process of investigations into the event's possible relation to the situation (or the myriad ways in which its consequences impact upon the world in question), this post-evental subject works to 'revolutionize' the situation in the gradual accretion of what mathematicians refer to as a *generic set*, which, as we will see in Chapter 5, is for Badiou the 'ontological schema' (or the elementary form) of any *truth*.

All of which leads us to the great big elephant in the room, namely, the unavoidable question: *what is a truth?*

Once again, perhaps the best way to go about answering this question is by first considering what it is *not*. For in Badiou's philosophy, truth – which, so far as he is concerned, is the sole quarry of philosophy – is not at all the result of an adequation between the thing-in-itself and its phenomenal or experiential representation. Nor, for that matter, is it a relative concept, shifting with the tide of opinion, nor a rule existing from time immemorial. Likewise, truth is neither a transcendent Idea, descending to us from on high, nor a revelation.

To the contrary, what truth *is* – or rather, what *a* truth is (there being, for Badiou, no such thing as a singular all-encompassing 'Truth', but rather only plural truths) – is something that is constructed from scratch, painstakingly built by a post-evental subject over the course of a truth-procedure, using only the matter of the world as its material. As such, far from being 'adequate', a truth – much like the procedure that underpins it – presents us with something fundamentally *exceptional*. For in issuing from a vanished event, a truth retains its forerunner's dominant characteristic, viz., its being radically subtracted from knowledge and thus an exception to all adequation.

More than this, rather than passively reflecting what *is*, a truth is something that radically *affects* knowledge and (it amounts to the same thing) power structures: far from being a qualification of knowledge or an intuition of the intelligible, a truth is something that bores a hole in knowledge. (Badiou again takes his cue from Lacan here, who famously held that truth 'hollows out its way into the real'[6] by punching a hole through knowledge.) Furthermore, while it is constructed piece by piece using only those resources ready at hand (and thereby remaining wholly immanent to the world in which it arises), a truth is nonetheless necessarily *incompletable*: even if the resources of the world in question were to dry up, the infinite nature of a truth means that there would always be, at least in principle, more to add. As such, a truth is never fully said.

Lastly and most importantly, every truth is, for complex reasons we will examine toward the end of this book, both *universal* and *eternal*, touching everything in the situation and extending even beyond that. Indeed, it is this characteristic that finally authorizes the name 'truth'. Again, this is a difficult point which involves complicated mathematical meditations on the nature of generic sets. We will therefore suffice ourselves for the moment by saying that a truth's universality results from its having no defining characteristic save what is common to everyone and everything (namely, the simple fact that it *is*), while its eternal nature lies in the fact that even if it disappears from one world, it can always reappear, or be 'resurrected', in another. Once established, a truth is available for all time.

Taking all these things together, we can now sketch out a preliminary 'check list' of the prerequisites of Badiou's concept of truth, observing that it must be, at one and the same time: radically *singular* (it is wholly un-known); epistemologically *affective* (it disrupts economies of knowledge); entirely *constructed* (it emerges *ex post facto* and requires militant support); and essentially *infinite* (it is necessarily incompletable). By the same token, it must also be *immanent* (it is a material construction taking place in a world); *eternal* (it is available for all time); and – fundamentally – *universal* (it is divorced from all particularity).

Given such extraordinarily demanding conditions, it should hardly come as a surprise that truths are not something we stumble across every day!

Dorothy the militant revolutionary

Before we conclude this introduction and move on to consider Badiou's peculiar formulation of being and appearing, let us take a moment to examine an example of a truth-procedure 'in action' by turning to Victor Fleming's classic 1939 film, *The Wizard of Oz*. For, outside of its apparently conservative, family-friendly appeal, Fleming's film arguably presents a fascinating filmic portrayal of what Badiou would call a *political truth-procedure*.

To begin with, let us remind ourselves of the obvious, that there are two fundamentally different yet interconnected worlds at play in *The Wizard of Oz*. This is a fairly uncontroversial point: anyone can see that the film is sharply divided between, on the one hand, the dull, monochromatic (and, fundamentally, 'static') world of Kansas; and on the other, the 'wonderful' technicolour Land of Oz. What I want to suggest here is that we understand the 'split' between these two worlds as being *evental* in nature; a division that is fundamentally one between a pre-evental world (Kansas) and its post-evental complement (Oz), with the tornado designating the divisive event itself.

Now, as we have seen, one of the essential characteristics of an event is that it takes place – if it takes place at all – in the 'voided' part of a situation. More precisely, an event happens on the 'edge of the void', what Badiou calls its *site*, lying at the outer limits of what is known by the state. In Badiou's philosophical jargon, the site constitutes a radically singular multiple, meaning that even though it is itself presented in the situation, none of the elements belonging to it are so fortunate. These elements are literally *unpresented* in the situation (or, more technically, they 'inappear' in the world in question).

Given that the site of the Kansas situation is clearly the farm on which Dorothy's Aunt and Uncle toil (together with their farmhands, Hunk, Zeke and Hickory), it is not such a great stretch to observe the properly voided element of this site to be *Dorothy herself*. In point of fact, Dorothy's voided position is explicitly announced in the opening of the film, when, in response to her desperate pleas to save Toto from imminent peril at the hands of Miss Gulch (who, in owning 'half the county', personifies statist rule, whose domination of the situation is beyond measure), Aunt Em forlornly explains to Dorothy that she 'can't go against the law'. The reality of the situation is however not simply that Dorothy cannot rail against the law *qua* state (or the law in the capacity of the state as Badiou defines it), but rather that, on a deeper (structural) level, she is unrecognized by the law *tout court*: devoid of all 'legal' representation, Dorothy literally *counts for nothing* in the state of Kansas. We might say that, according to this world's logic, Dorothy does not in fact exist. Rather, she *inexists*.

The celebrated tornado – certainly one of the most iconic filmic representations of the void's coming ferociously and fleetingly to life (what is a tornado if not a void momentarily given powerful physical form?) – thus dramatizes the event itself, through which Kansas' proper inexistent suddenly attains a maximal degree of existence, a 'surging forth' that is visually represented as Dorothy (whose surname, 'Gale' nominally indexes her to this void) is swept high into the vortex. So too is it at this point that the previously immeasurable domination of the state over its situation – such immeasurability being, we recall, a key ontological characteristic in Badiou's philosophy – is given a precise measure, a delimitation of power metaphorically enacted in the exposure of Miss Gulch as the Wicked Witch of the West (the indexing of statist excess to 'the West' also being of no small significance). It is to this initial eventual measuring of statist power that Badiou gives the name 'political prescription'.

When Dorothy emerges to confide in Toto that 'we're not in Kansas anymore', we are left in little doubt that a revolution is taking place: the Wicked Witch of the East (*qua* oppressive state power) has been crushed by a farmhouse (along with its concomitant Marxist connotations) and the situation has been irrevocably transformed. Bleak mid-western America gives way to the Wonderful World of Oz; dull monochrome is replaced by vibrant technicolour; the previously unrepresented/inexistent Dorothy suddenly finds herself the person who exists most intensely in the world; and Dorothy's arduous investigatory process begins.

Indeed, to stretch the revolutionary metaphor even further, the Yellow Brick Road – the effective 'path of truth' that stretches out over the whole of Oz – itself originates in a spiral (much like the tornado-event itself), connoting as much its voided point of origin (the spiral extending from an imperceptible point, a point 'beyond' both presentation and representation) as its (at least potentially) infinite extension (Figure 1).

Figure 1. Still from *The Wizard of Oz* (1939).

Dorothy's progress can then be read in terms of militant or 'faithful' subjectivity, inasmuch as she engages in an arduous truth-procedure, setting out along the Yellow Brick Road – a path traversing the entire land of Oz, painstakingly laid out brick by brick and dotted with intersections or 'points' (another key Badiouian term we will explore later in this book) at which pure directional decisions (left or right? East or west?) must be made – so as to demand from the state her due.

And so during her investigations in the land of Oz she garners an endearing collection of essentially Marxist metaphors: a heartless Tin Man (symbolizing the forces of production); a Cowardly Lion who dreams of becoming 'King' (representing the politician, or, on a more Leninist note, the party); and, of course, a brainless Scarecrow (representing the figure of the worker, who, in proper Marxist fashion, warrants most attention: recall Dorothy's parting words to Scarecrow; 'I think I'll miss you most of all!'). Being that each of these figures find themselves connected in one way or another to the Kansas-event, coupled with the fact that they are composed from the material that made up the site itself (namely, the farmhands Hunk, Zeke and Hickory), we might call this fledgling party 'the militants of the Kansas-event'.

Taken together, our militants constitute what Badiou would call a new 'subject-body', created in the wake of the Kansas-event. It is between this new body and the trace of the vanished Kansas-event – this trace being none other than *Dorothy herself*, the former inexistent who now exists absolutely and loudly proclaims the possibility of what was hitherto impossible (Scarecrow *can* have a brain, Tin Man *can* have a heart, Lion *can* have courage), and whose sole desire is simply to return home – that a new *political subject* is born.

And so, after a series of decisional points and state-related challenges, our militants finally reach the Emerald City (the bourgeois connotations of which are obvious) to demand certain situational changes – changes which roughly echo the path famously mapped out by Marx and Engels in *The Communist Manifesto* – in the form of *brains* (signifying less 'intelligence' than 'class consciousness', designating the coming-into-being of the proletariat); *hearts* (broadly symbolic of 'generic humanity', the realization of which lies in the final overcoming of the 'inhumane' contradiction at the heart of the relations of production); *courage* (understood as militancy, facilitating the coming of the dictatorship of the proletariat); and, most importantly, *home* (representing equal membership in the situation, that is, the ultimate dissolution of the proletarian dictatorship in the realization of a finally classless society).

The metaphorical nature of our militants together with their demands should leave us in no doubt whatsoever that these requests are pitched at a universal level ('brains *for-all*', 'courage *for-all*', 'hearts *for all*', 'home *for-all*'). In point of fact, the universal truth induced from the situation of Oz after the Kansas-event is nothing less than the properly political truth of *absolute equality*. For what is Dorothy's demand for a home, for a proper place, if not the egalitarian axiom that everybody deserves equal footing in the situation, that everyone should be legally recognized and nobody should be excluded (or, in Marxist terms, that a communist society must be realized, here and now)?

Yet if there is one thing the state cannot tolerate, it is the idea of real equality. Thus Dorothy's political prescription must ultimately be brought to bear on the 'real' head of state when, after their egalitarian requests are flatly rejected by the giant head of Oz – 'Oz' being both the literal and figurative embodiment of the 'head of *state*' (the synonymity of his name with the land itself not being lost here) – the militants of the Kansas event once again 'measure the immeasurable', drawing back the curtains obscuring Oz and thereby (quite literally) cutting him down to size. Thus Oz is revealed to be neither wizard nor giant head, but rather a doddering old man, and the situation is accordingly radicalized: Oz the man (*qua* 'measured' state) abandons rule to the militants of the Kansas-event, spelling (in classical Marxist terms) the transitional dictatorship of the proletariat, and as the film closes we safely assume that the whole of Oz will live happily ever after.

Thus we see how *The Wizard of Oz* contains the basic outline of what Badiou calls a truth-procedure, whereby an event, emanating from an obscure site that is fundamentally unpresented within the situation, suddenly and unpredictably flashes in and out of existence, rupturing with (and thereby giving the measure of) the state and its regime of repetition by affirming the possibility of something radically *new*, the full consequences of which are only afterward painstakingly drawn out by a new subject who, born in the wake of this vanished event, traverses and in so doing transforms the entire situation through the construction of a *new universal truth*.

PART ONE

Being and appearing

Chapter 1
Unframing, enframing, reframing

So far, we have focused almost exclusively on the 'radical' side of Badiou's thought, the part comprising the *event* and everything that follows from its sudden irruption, and which is preoccupied with things like newness and sweeping change. Yet Badiou's so-called 'mature' philosophy effectively kicks off long before the event arrives on the scene, with his celebrated (if initially perplexing) pronouncement in the opening pages of *Being and Event* that 'mathematics *is* ontology'.[1]

It really is difficult to overstate the importance of this inaugural assertion. Everything that follows from it – from the structure of situations and their states all the way to events and the subjects and truths they can engender – must be understood as the carefully drawn out consequences of this initial philosophical *decision* (we say 'decision' because the actual mathematical status of ontology is, as we will see, not something that can be *known*, but rather something that can only be *decided upon*). In fact, as we suggested at the very start of this book, such is the rigor with which Badiou constructs *Being and Event* that those who reject Badiou's core philosophy arguably do so foremost because they reject his initial thesis on the equivalence of mathematics and ontology. For if this thesis is unfounded, so too is Badiou's entire philosophy. Conversely, in accepting the equivalence of mathematics and ontology it is hard to avoid its manifold ramifications, meticulously laid out in *Being and Event* and the works that follow.

The one or the multiple?

Before we consider the meaning (much less the consequences) of Badiou's equation of ontology with mathematics, we would do well to remind ourselves exactly what ontology is.

Plainly put, ontology designates the science of being *qua* being. This was Aristotle's original definition in the *Metaphysics*, and Badiou employs it as such in his own writings. Yet 'being' is itself an elusive concept. The easiest way to come to grips with it is through a simple thought experiment. First, imagine an object, any object; a tree, another person, a wooden stool, a paper bag... Now imagine that we can strip away all of this object's properties, everything that identifies the object as *this* object (and not another). All we can now say of the object is that it simply *is*. This indistinct remainder is none other than the object's pure *being*. 'Being *qua* being' (meaning being *itself* or being *as such*) is then basically another way of saying *pure being*, or being that purely and simply *is*, divorced from all of its particular qualities and attributes. Moreover, given that everything that exists *is*, ontology would seem to equally designate the study of what is common to everything. In this precise sense – and this will become important later in the book – ontology is equally the discourse of universality.

It is also essential to recognize that when Badiou says that ontology literally *is* mathematics, this is in no way to suggest that being is itself mathematical or is composed of mathematical objects. To the contrary, what he means is that mathematics figures the scientific discourse on, or way of talking about, being. (Accordingly, to suggest that being is itself mathematical would be to illegitimately conflate ontology, which is simply the discourse on being, with the object of this discourse, namely, *being itself*.) Or more precisely, mathematics says everything that can be said about being; it is the only discourse up to the task of articulating being *qua* being. It is however, for reasons we will explore presently, only today – which is to say, after

Georg Cantor's invention of the mathematical field of set theory in the late nineteenth century (and its subsequent axiomatization by Ernst Zermelo and Abraham Fraenkel in the early twentieth century) – that we can truly know this.

Mathematics to one side, in *Being and Event* Badiou holds that being itself, being *qua* being, is nothing other than *pure multiplicity*. By which he means that once an object is divested of (or subtracted from) everything that goes into making it a 'unique' thing – once we isolate it from its context and strip away all of its qualitative determinations – what remains is essentially a multiple of multiples. There is no intrinsic determination to this multiple multiplicity; it is not a multiple of 'this' or of 'that', rather, it is purely – or it purely *is* – multiple. This pure multiple remainder, Badiou claims, is precisely the *being* of the object, the elementary 'there is' underlying everything that 'is there'. Crucially, there is no 'atomic' halting point to this infinite decomposition; what we arrive at is not the 'One' (that is, some form of primordial unity, an indivisible base from which everything sallies forth), but rather the void, nothingness itself – the in-finite dissemination of multiple multiplicity.

Now, if the idea that in journeying to the heart of 'what is' we do not eventually stumble across some elementary unit – a kind of irreducible 'atom of being' – but rather only infinite multiple multiplicity seems somewhat counterintuitive, well, that's because it is. Indeed, Badiou begins *Being and Event* by literally turning the history of ontology – which, from Parmenides on, holds that what *is* is one and what is *there* (or is presented) is multiple – on its head.

Taking as his point of departure Plato's famous theses on the one and the multiple in the *Parmenides*, Badiou begins by isolating a crucial variation in Plato's terminology – specifically, between two 'kinds' of multiplicity, πληθος (*plethos*) and πολλα (*polla*) – to argue that Plato's true position is not, as it is generally understood, that 'if the one is not, nothing is', but rather that 'if the one is not, (the) nothing is'.² The logic here is subtle but no less devastating. At base it means that, if there is no ultimate consistency or unity to being ('if the one *is not...*'), then being must in fact *in-consist* ('...the nothing *is*'). This simple but counter-intuitive reversal is really the key to Badiou's 'subtractive' ontology: that which is one (or is 'consistent') is not, strictly speaking, what *is*. Rather, what *is per se* is multiple (devoid of any instance of the one, radically withdrawn from all possible unification). Which is finally to say that being, when thought *in its very being* (that is, as being *qua* being), is nothing other than inconsistent multiplicity, and that ontology, which is the discourse on being, must accordingly be the science of the *pure multiple*.

So Badiou launches his philosophical project by arguing against the one in favour of the multiple which is radically 'without-one' (recruiting Plato to his cause along the way). Yet he cannot escape the fact that 'oneness' exists, that even things that are multiple are nevertheless presented to us *as* unified. For unity is something that is repeatedly testified to by our everyday experiences; simply, each and every object we experience is, in an immediate sense, discrete and coherent, that is to say, *unified* (when was the last time you experienced the 'multiple-without-one'?!). Intuitively, this means that even though, technically speaking, the one *is not*, there is nevertheless an 'effect' of oneness, a 'one-effect' whereby inconsistency is somehow rendered consistent. This *uni*fication or 'one-ification' of pure multiplicity is precisely the *presentation* of multiplicity as such. Or again, while pure multiplicity is itself inconsistent, it is nonetheless *presented* as unified. Badiou calls such unified presentation a *situation*. One of the most plastic and immediately useful terms in Badiou's philosophical lexicon, a situation is thus *any presented multiplicity whatsoever*: the desk at which I am currently sitting, the city of Bremen, several sunflowers in a vase, a gathering of sea urchins off the Florida coast, the ruins of ancient Greece, an art exhibition, Brazil, a political demonstration, Picasso's *Guernica*, the discourse of ontology itself...

Now the operation by which pure multiplicity actually becomes 'one-ified' (i.e. is presented or 'situated') is itself termed the 'count-as-one' or simply the *count*, for the rather straightforward reason that it 'counts' certain elements (multiples) as *belonging* to the situation (while at the same time 'discounting' others). The count is thus the operation that *structures* the situation – indeed, it literally *is* the structure of the situation – and is to this effect indistinguishable from the situation itself. The crucial ontological distinction is then found at the level of the situation's being: the pure being of the situation – the 'before of the count' (or what precedes structuration) – necessarily remains beyond the situation itself, inasmuch as its being is *uncounted* (or 'inconsistent') multiplicity.

The paradox here is fundamental: as all knowledge is necessarily 'situated', the in-consistent being which underlies all consistency is itself radically unknowable. Thus any consideration of what precedes the situation is itself hopelessly compromised *by virtue of its very situatedness*. Inconsistency is therefore what Lacan would call the 'real' of presentation, namely, the point at which knowledge butts against its own limit. Which is why Badiou's initial embrace of the multiple (and concurrent assertion that 'the one *is not*') is moreover a *pure* decision, insofar as the actual status of pure multiplicity is itself properly *undecidable*. Furthermore, this is one of the main reasons why Badiou's ontology should be understood as being essentially *subtractive*: in the face of a classical metaphysics defined by 'the *enframing* of being by the one',[3] Badiou decides that ontology can be nothing other than the theory of in-different, in-consistent multiplicity, radically subtracted from the power of the one. (We will return to this 'subtractive' point momentarily.)

And so, with a simple yet powerful philosophical gesture, Badiou *unframes* being and returns it to its originary abstraction.

The void and the state

While these difficult and demanding meditations on the one and the multiple may leave you fighting a strong urge to pour yourself a stiff drink, we need to exercise just a little more fortitude as there are two very important consequences of this ontological abstraction that must be highlighted before we can move on. The first is the problem of the *void*, while the second is its ostensible 'solution' in the form of the *state*.

As we have seen, it follows from the fact that the situation and the count are one and the same thing that the inconsistent substructure of a situation is itself fundamentally ungraspable. However, the simple fact that the count is itself an operation tells us that there must be something on which this operation operates (as we can hardly have an operation without there being something operated-upon!). Thus the count, by its very nature, retroactively posits a corollary 'to-be-counted', a 'before-of-the-count' that can be said to 'in-consist' in the situation.

Now, given the seemingly self-contradictory fact that, whilst everything is counted, the count itself necessarily posits a kind of 'phantom remainder' (namely, the initial multiple *qua* inconsistent being of the situation), we can only conclude that while the pure multiple is *excluded* from the situation – from presentation itself – it must at the same time be *included* in the presentation 'in-itself'. Excluded from presentation itself, included in presentation in-itself, the pure multiple must really *be nothing* in the situation. Yet as Badiou points out, being-nothing is not at all the same thing as non-being. In fact, this 'nothing' subsists within the situation in two immediate guises: in the very operation of the count (which, in its 'pure transparency', remains itself uncounted); and in the pure multiple upon which the count operates (which, as we have seen, differs in itself from its situated, or consistent, result). The pure multiple thus 'in-consists' within the situation in the form of the *void* – as the void *in situ* – and as such figures the precise point at which the situation is 'sutured' to its inconsistent being.

Two immediate and important theses follow from this proposition: first, that, according to the situation, the void is the proper name of being; and second, that everything that *is* is woven from the void.

Yet even while existence owes all that it is to the void, the latter nonetheless presents a real danger to the situation, inasmuch as its very in-consistency inevitably threatens the fabric of structured presentation. For were the situation to actually encounter its void – were it to paradoxically *present* its inherent inconsistency – this would necessarily undermine its own consistency and thereby spell the 'ruin of the one'. Accordingly, so as to avoid such a catastrophe, every situation as a matter of course subjects itself to a structural re-count, a 'count of the count' whereby the initial count is itself counted (for, as we saw above, what escapes the operation of the count is precisely the count itself). This essential *reframing* of the situation establishes a kind of metastructure ensuring that everything in the situation is present and accounted for.

It is this double structuration by which the structure of a situation is itself 'counted as one' – thereby ensuring that there is both *presentation* and *representation* (or, if you prefer, 'enframing' and 'reframing') – that Badiou calls, for its 'metaphorical affinity with politics',[4] the *state of the situation* (or simply the 'state'). Furthermore, it is in this precise sense that Badiou can say that in our world 'what counts – in the sense of what is valued – is that which is counted'.[5]

These three successional acts of framing – the *unframing* of the one (inconsistent or pure multiplicity), the *enframing* of being (situation), and the *reframing* of the situation (state) – are the grounds on which Badiou constructs his entire philosophical edifice.

The art of subtraction

While it is not especially hard to see the enormously productive role of Badiou's ontology – its vast edifice being entirely built, as we have seen, out of operations that are essentially performed on *nothing* (i.e. the void) – we need to keep in mind how its basic gesture is in fact *subtractive*. Indeed, as indicated above, Badiou's ontology is first and foremost a 'subtractive ontology'. We can understand this in a number of ways.

First, it is subtractive in that it in no way purports to convey being as presence. Being (*qua* being) is most assuredly not what is presented to us. To the contrary, being – *pure being* – is that which defies any and every form of presentation (or representation, for that matter). Radically withdrawn from all unification, being is nothing other than uncounted – and therefore unpresented – multiplicity. Which moreover implies that Badiou's ontology is also subtractive in a second sense, in that it subtracts (or 'unframes') being from its capture by the one of unification (which is, as we have seen, the dominant trope of classical metaphysics).

Perhaps most importantly however, Badiou's ontology is subtractive in that its fundamental gesture, curiously enough, is to subtract *being itself* from ontology. For ontology is ultimately a discourse that prescribes the rules by which something can be presented or counted as one – its sole operation being that of the count – and the one thing that *fails* to be counted as a matter of course is nothing other than inconsistent multiplicity, or *being itself*. So, technically speaking, and contrary to what we might reasonably expect, being is not actually given in ontology; rather, it is retroactively posited on the basis of conceiving the one as a 'result' (of the operation of the count). Pure multiplicity, as we have already said, is then not something that can be *known* (or again, while we certainly know that being *is*, we cannot know *what* it is); rather, the nature of being is something that must be *decided* upon, in an axiomatic sense.

Subtraction is thus an extremely important feature of Badiou's ontology, as well as of his philosophy more broadly. It is moreover a process that is visibly at work – and in much the same manner – in a great deal of the art of the past century. Badiou even goes so far as to argue that subtraction – taken as a strategic means of attaining to 'the real', or to the brute essence of reality, its seemingly indivisible and inaccessible core – can be taken as a defining axiom of the art of the twentieth century. For just as with Badiou's ontology, what such art attempts first and foremost is to do away with the pretence of semblance or false appearance, and in this manner cut through the deceiving layers of 'reality' so as to arrive at something truly (and often disturbingly) *real*. Or more accurately, the ultimate aim of such art is not to capture the real itself – which, as we have seen, is as unknowable as it is unpresentable – but rather to present the constitutive *gap* between semblance and the real, between constitutive reality and its inconsistent underside (or, ontologically speaking, between presentation and its underlying being).

This is in fact precisely how Badiou interprets the great modernist project for a 'pure art': as less a demand for the 'autonomization' of the arts and the exclusive commitment to their own medium (where artistic form is placed entirely at the service of the specific medium and is pursued to its so-called logical end, as in the popular 'Greenbergian' conception of modernism),[6] than for an art in which the sole function of *semblance* – which, we should bear in mind, is for Badiou ultimately what art truly *is* – would be to signify 'the rawness of the real'.[7] Or in other words, all of the great art of the twentieth century can be seen to bear witness to a desire to lay bare the very void that gives consistency to reality itself.

Of the countless examples of such a subtractive art – of an art that literally (or more precisely, *figuratively*, i.e. through figures) presents the constitutive gap between the real and semblance – there is perhaps none more striking than Kasimir Malevich's seminal suprematist painting *White on White* (1918; Figure 2). Badiou himself holds Malevich's work up as the epitome of purification within the field of painting, in addition to marking the origin of the subtractive orientation of thought that would become one of the defining features of the twentieth century.

Figure 2. Kasimir Malevich, *White on White* (1918).

In the painting itself Malevich experiments with the furthest reaches of abstraction: a white square is suspended above a white field, its contours barely discernable from its surroundings, its form hovering at the very threshold of visibility. There is no reference whatsoever to external reality, only the asymmetrical square floating silently in the void. Everything in the painting has been systematically evacuated: form is sacrificed and colour has been almost totally drained, leaving only a pale geometrical allusion, 'the zero of form', little more than the *idea* of a square.

Yet it is precisely this bare geometrical allusion – this 'pure remainder' – which encapsulates the very essence of the subtractive procedure that we have been discussing. Everything having been evacuated, what Malevich's white square provides is in effect the bare support for a minimal difference, namely, 'the abstract difference of ground and form, and above all, the null difference between white and white, the difference of the Same'.[8] Put another way, what *White on White* so perfectly presents, in the realm of art, and through entirely subtractive means, is the gap between the bare minimum effect of structure (the fragile white square) and that which is radically unstructured (the white void). Or in ontological terms: *White on White* presents the gap between the operation of the count and the abyss of pure multiplicity; between structural consistency and the formlessness of the void; between the situation and its in-consistent underside.

At the same time however, we can say that this gap also figures a point of radical *indiscernibility*, a point where multiple-being and its counting-as-one (the white square being, after all, perhaps *the* paradigmatic instance of a 'unit') are brought so close as to become indistinguishable from each other. So by placing form at the edge of the void, 'in a network of cuts and disappearances',[9] Malevich's painting effectively captures the abstract difference between being itself and what is presented of being. It is to this effect that we can say of Malevich's *White on White* that it truly is an ontological painting.

We might further clarify this subtractive process by which pure being is extracted from structured presentation by turning, briefly and in a very general sense, to the art of drawing. In doing so, we should first note that contemporary drawing (so far as Badiou conceives it) is entirely concerned with producing a point at which being and what is presented of being – or where the real and its semblance – are rendered indiscernible. For unlike painting, drawing is *by its very nature* a minimalist art, relying not on the strength of its means but rather on the meagre effect of a few lines and marks, lines which only exist insofar as they are composed on a (for all intents and purposes) blank surface.

Yet we must at the same time recognize how the surface which provides the drawing's material support (be it a piece of paper, an illuminated screen, an expanse of wall, or whatever...) is equally, in a very real sense, itself brought into existence by these minimal lines and marks, by virtue of the fact that they effectively create the background *as* an open space. So we have in drawing, at one and the same time, two fundamentally opposed existential supports: on the one hand, the blank surface pre-exists the lines and marks as a closed totality, which themselves only come into being inasmuch as they are presented within its space; while on the other, it is the lines and marks that establish this open surface as such, retroactively giving form to the (empty) background by designating it *as* a place of presentation.

Drawing thus involves a kind of 'movable reciprocity between existence and inexistence',[10] an indiscernible exchange that designates in turn the fundamental *fragility* of drawing. The whole art of drawing, according to Badiou, then revolves around capturing and displaying this delicate exchange between existence and inexistence, or between consistency and in-consistency, by fixing (in a manner not entirely dissimilar to Malevich's subtractive painting) a point of indiscernibility between figure and ground, whereby the marks themselves are barely discernible from their background. Or again, by tracing a line, however faint, between what *is* and what *is there*.

From mathematical ontology to logical phenomenology

It is however important to recognize that the subtractive tendency visibly at work in modern art does not, properly speaking, 'condition' Badiou's own subtractive ontology (we will come back to this key concept of 'conditioning' in the following chapter). So for example, while Badiou points out how drawing immediately seizes the definition of being as pure multiplicity by reducing any and every thing to a simple system of marks, this is not to suggest that his actual concept of pure multiplicity is itself in some way drawn from art (although, as we will see in Part Two, art does have a crucial extra-mathematical or supplementary role to play in his ontology).

To the contrary – and again, it really is hard to overstate this point – Badiou *entirely equates mathematics with ontology*. As we have already seen, this is the 'radical' thesis that both opens *Being and Event* and determines its overall trajectory (as well as that of his philosophy as a whole), namely, that mathematics – or more precisely, Zermelo-Fraenkel set theory (ZFC), the axiomatic system that purports to offer a solid foundation for mathematics[11] – *is* ontology.

Now, as we have already said, this is in no way to declare that being is itself mathematical, nor is it to suggest that mathematics somehow discovers or 'reveals' ontology. It simply means that ontology – which, as we know, figures the *discourse* on being *qua* being – is *exactly the same thing as mathematics*; so far as Badiou is concerned, to 'do' mathematics is precisely the same as to 'do' ontology. As such, working mathematicians are themselves, consciously or unconsciously, to the last one, essentially practical ontologists. One of the more interesting and immediate consequences of this radical equation of ontology with mathematics is that philosophy finds itself cut off from what would otherwise be considered its privileged discourse. For while mathematics effectively 'writes' being (inasmuch as it *is* ontology), philosophy can itself only speak 'metaontologically'. Or again, whereas mathematics is the practice of directly inscribing pure multiplicity (which, for Badiou, is precisely what being *is*), philosophy can only offer second-order considerations on the nature of being (hence it's 'meta' status).

So why then, to return to the question we raised at the beginning of this chapter, is mathematics ontology? Because, Badiou says, mathematics and mathematics alone 'makes truth out of the pure multiple'.[12] Or in other words, because mathematics provides the minimal and sufficient structure necessary to articulate multiple multiplicity. Indeed, Zermelo-Fraenkel set theory literally 'thinks' pure multiplicity in a number of immediate ways. For one thing, a set in ZFC has no 'essence' other than that of being a multiple; it is determined neither externally (nothing constrains the way it seizes another thing) nor internally (a set is entirely indifferent to what it collects). Meaning a set, thought in itself, *in-consists*: it consists (or is composed) of nothing, its sole predicate being its multiple nature. To this end a set literally *is* inconsistent multiplicity. What is more, every element of a set is itself a set, meaning every multiple is itself a multiple of multiples, without reference to any unitary element. So a set *qua* inconsistent multiplicity is radically without-one; it is, in its essence, uncounted multiple multiplicity.

In point of fact, everything that we have examined thus far on the side of both inconsistency (pure multiplicity, presentation in-itself, operation of the count) and consistency (impure or 'one-ified' multiplicity, presentation itself, counted situation), as well as that which bleeds between the two (the void), finds an immediate correlate in ZFC. A situation (*qua* consistent multiple), for example, is literally a set, inasmuch as a set, in its most elementary definition, is simply 'a plurality thought as a unit'.[13] Likewise, the second-order 'reframing' of the situation (the structural re-count or 'count of the count' that constitutes the 'state' of the situation) finds mathematical expression in the axiom of the power set, which essentially tells us that, for every set χ, there also exists a set of all the subsets of χ (we will return to this decisive axiom in our discussion of the event and the subject in Part Two). Moreover, ZFC admits of only one true relation, *belonging* (written $\in$), which alone dictates what composes or one-ifies (or 'enframes') a set, meaning the set itself (*qua* multiple) possesses no 'unary predicate', no essence other than its being a multiple.

So too set theory, through the axiom of the void set, premises existence itself on the void, that is, on the empty or memberless set, on the set to which no elements belong (written Ø). Thus, rather than affirming a 'first' multiple from which all other multiples are derived (and thereby illegally smuggling the one back into being at the level of the multiple) or designating origination at the point of the multiple-counted-as-one (thus overlooking the count's status as *result*), set theory contrarily substantializes the very 'nothing' affecting the purity of the multiple, that is, it literally makes this nothing *be* through the assumption of a proper name (the void, Ø).[14]

Still, in its reduction to questions of *essence* – to the question of being in its 'integral transparency', or to 'the flat surface of indifferent multiplicity'[15] – Badiou's mathematical ontology proves to be wholly incapable of accounting for exactly how it is that different multiples can come to *appear* or 'be *there*' with varying degrees of intensity in different situations. For in set theory, either something *belongs*, or it does not; there are no nuances or gradations to (re)presentation. So for example, either $\beta \in \alpha$, meaning β absolutely belongs to α, or $\beta \notin \alpha$, in which case β forms no part whatsoever of α. Moreover, while relationality is obviously a fundamental characteristic of appearing – every '*there*' being 'the product of a particular set of differential relations that flesh out a situation in a particular way'[16] – there can be no properly differential or relational thought to being, as one of set theory's fundamental axioms (that of *extensionality*) only allows for absolute difference and absolute identity: either two multiples possess exactly the same elements (and are therefore the same) or they do not (and are accordingly absolutely different).

It is therefore not enough to understand a situation simply as a multiple/set. Rather, one needs to take into account the entire network of relations it sustains. Or again: since the mathematical theory of pure multiplicity only provides the thought of *presentation as such* (and no more), there needs to be some way to think everything that *is presented* (or 'appears') in the infinity of the real situation itself.

It just so happens, however, that there is a branch of mathematics that thinks such relationality, namely, the field of mathematical or mathematized *logic*. Accordingly, in solving this and other problems Badiou's recent work has moved from a singular ontology that identifies situations in terms of their strict multiple-neutrality, to a broader onto-*logical* conception of *being-there*, which has both a mathematical and a *logical* side, and which accounts for the 'contamination' of being with its phenomenal appearing (or its differential localization in a world).[17] Hence the parallel thesis governing his third 'great book', *Logics of Worlds*: just as mathematics (formalized by post-Cantorian set theory) thinks the purity of being, so too logic – or more precisely, *category theory* (in particular the difficult branches that deal with topoi and sheaves) – thinks appearing or being-there-in-a-world.

Before we dive headlong into the depths of Badiou's logical phenomenology however, let us take a moment to consider another artistic example that in many ways provides the immediate counterpoint to Malevich's *White on White*, this being Mark Rothko's 1954 painting *Ochre and Red on Red* (Figure 3).

One of the first things we notice when we compare these two paintings is how, while Rothko's painting-world (for the painting is indeed a *world*) can equally be seen to evacuate itself of almost all content, far from exhausting the image and confronting us with the bare minimum of formal means (as in Malevich's subtractive work), Rothko contrarily saturates his canvas with colour, layering it in such a way as to suggest the light were radiating out from within – from some hidden internal source (what he called its 'inner light') – presenting us with something closer to pure intensities of colour. Whereas Malevich's painting eliminates form, colour and space to the point where only a pale

Figure 3. Mark Rothko, *Ochre and Red on Red* (1954).

geometrical allusion remains, here these dimensions are not so much excluded as gradually evoked or suggested, as if summoned into existence by the painting itself. In Rothko's work form is not reduced to the vacuum of the void, but is rather induced from it bit by bit.

While employing similarly subtractive means, Rothko's painting nonetheless accomplishes something very different to Malevich's: if, in the realm of art, *White on White* captures the abstract difference between being itself and what is presented of being, *Ochre and Red on Red* contrarily presents us with *presentation itself*. Or again, Rothko's painting leads us not to the edge of the void, but rather to a place of pure appearing.

The contrasting methods of Malevich and Rothko – which we are here equating respectively to an ontological and a properly logical approach – are moreover not entirely dissimilar to the dual subtractive procedures of 'separation' and 'isolation' Badiou identifies as being at work in the poetry of Stéphane Mallarmé (who we will encounter again later in this book). Indeed, Badiou spends much time teasing out the intricacies of Mallarmé's dual operations in *Conditions*, demonstrating how 'isolation' consists in 'bringing forth a contour of nothingness that extirpates the given from any nearness to what it is not',[18] and thereby allows us to pass from the counted or 'consistent' multiple to its pure multiple-being; whereas 'separation' contrarily involves 'cutting out' a multiple in order to establish a scene wherein everything that belongs to it might be enumerated and catalogued, thereby bringing about 'the purified consciousness of a [...] detotalized multiple'.[19]

Or in other words, 'isolation' involves an absolute de-relation or purification (all proximities and connections to the thing are gradually suppressed or suspended until we arrive at the ideal purity of the thing-in-itself), while 'separation' performs an absolute subtraction (the thing itself is cut from its surroundings and gradually brought into heightened focus).

Obviously *White on White* provides us with a clear-cut instance of isolation: everything in the world of the painting is evacuated (form, content, colour...) leaving only an absolutely minimal difference, the 'difference of the Same' which, as we have seen, figures the gap between the bare minimum effect of structure and the infinite abyss of pure multiplicity. *Ochre and Red on Red* on the other hand is a work of separation through and through: here colour itself is subtracted from its 'true' context and presented in the world of the painting as hazy blocks of vibrant, almost vital (or as the artist himself would say, 'sublime') intensity. Vacillating between figure and ground, Rothko's rectangular blocks of colour are neither discreet (as in formalist abstract art) nor indistinguishable (as in Malevich's painting); rather, colour and form emerge on the canvas – purely and uncomplicatedly – as if from a single, undifferentiated source.

In direct contrast to Malevich's ascetic work, Rothko presents us not with multiple-being but rather pure appearing in the form of pure colour: a world of colour that is at once the colour of the world.

Logics of worlds

Returning to Badiou's logical phenomenology, we might now ask ourselves: what exactly is a world? There is in fact a very simple (if slightly imprecise) answer to this question: it is a *situation in which beings appear*.

To explain: while a world is, like a situation, *essentially* a multiple of multiples (indeed, ontologically speaking, it *is* a situation), these multiples are also caught up in a complex relational network according to which they 'appear' more or less intensely with regard to one another. These differentially appearing multiplicities moreover constitute the *objects* of a world, which is to say that a multiple's worldly appearing is ultimately equivalent to its objectification: appearance is literally the 'becoming-object' of the multiple. So it would seem that Malevich's famous pronouncement that 'each form is a world'[20] holds a deep philosophical truth: just as every object must take place in a world, so too do these objects constitute worlds unto themselves.

The relative intensity of an object's appearing in a world then falls under the jurisdiction of the *transcendental* immanent to that world. This naturally begs the question: what is a transcendental? Once again, the ontological answer is straightforward enough: it is a partially ordered set belonging to the situation ('partial ordering' referring, somewhat intuitively, to a set whose elements are arranged in a specific order). However, as the transcendental's function rests with appearing (given that, as we have said, it is responsible for regulating the variable intensities of appearance of a world's manifold objects), it must be accounted for in logical terms. To do so, we need first note that, just as a situation is a set, so too a world constitutes a *topos* (or to be more precise, a specific kind of topos known as a *Grothendieck topos*). Which of course leads us to ask: what is a topos? Well, in extremely reductive terms, it is a category of topological space that behaves in a manner strikingly similar to that of sets (save the emphasis on functions or morphisms over belonging), whose terms are objects and their relations, and which contains finite limits, exponentials, and a subobject classifier.

Now, accepting for the moment that a topos is indeed the logical articulation of a world (just as a set is the ontological articulation of a situation), we can with relative ease equate its finite limits with the boundaries of the world, exponentials with its various objects, and the subobject classifier with the world's transcendental. Without going into too much detail, the finite limits of a topos involve both a *terminal* and an *initial* object. The terminal object, also designated 'One', effectively envelops the entirety of the topos (or the transcendental regime of the world in question), meaning that every object of the topos 'counts as one' only inasmuch as it enters into a relationship with this 'One'. The initial object, on the other hand, which is also designated 'Zero', is an object which fails to enter into any relation with the terminal object (or, for that matter, any of the other objects), and as such is not 'counted as one'. We can of course easily discern a certain homology between this initial or 'Zero' object (which fails to be 'counted as one') and the empty or void set of ontology proper. Further, the point of convergence of the manifold relations between all of the subobjects of a topos is the topos' *subobject classifier*, which acts rather as it sounds, serving to classify all the subobjects of the topos in question (of which it itself is equally a subobject). And to finally answer our initial question, it is precisely this 'central object' which enjoys a relation with every object (save the initial object) of the topos-world that Badiou designates the *transcendental* of a world.

Now, given that a world (*qua* topos) constitutes a site of appearing, and appearing is meted out in varying degrees of *intensity* (certain things appear more or less intensely than others), clearly the key to a world's logic lies in its being *ordered*. This intensive ordering – which is ultimately the function of the transcendental of the world in question – in effect involves the evaluation of each and every object's relation to all the other objects of the world (including itself). As such, it is thought *differentially*, in terms of identities and differences, on an asymmetrical scale of 'more or less'. Such 'transcendental evaluation' is understood in terms of *indexing* (inasmuch as evaluating a world's objects involves 'indexing' them to its transcendental). As Badiou rather succinctly puts it:

if x and y are two elements of a being A, and T is the transcendental of the world in question, indexing is an identity-function **Id**(x, y) which measures in T the degree of 'apparent' identity between x and y. In other words, if **Id**$(x, y) = p$, it means that x and y are 'identical to the p degree' with regard to their power of appearance in the world.[21]

Thought outside of its multiple-being, indexing constitutes a multiple's *phenomenon*. Badiou reserves the name *object* for the couple formed by a multiple's phenomenon (its transcendental indexing) and the multiple itself. Meaning that an object of a world is ultimately nothing other than the transcendental indexing of a multiple, thought simultaneously in its being *and* its appearing.

Given the precondition of a topos' being closed – that is, its demand for both an initial and a terminal object ('Zero' and 'One') – we will say of a world's transcendental regime that there is both a *minimum* degree (absolute difference, or **Id**$(x, y) = \mu$) and a *maximum* degree (absolute identity, or **Id**(x, y) = *M*), together with the manifold *p* degrees that fall between these extremes. A world's transcendental regime therefore requires that there be not only an absolutely apparent object (i.e. an object that enjoys a maximal degree of identity between itself and every other object that appears in the world), but also posits its opposite, namely, an object which has a 'zero-degree of appearance', one which fails to 'identify' (or enter into a relationship) with any other worldly object. Being identical to nothing in the world, such an object will be said to *inappear* in the world in question. By the same token, the object that enjoys the maximal transcendental degree will be said to be *absolutely there*.

Which brings us finally and ineluctably to the question of *existence*. What exactly is it to exist? Given everything that we have seen thus far – that ontology is the science of the pure multiple; that being-there is the logical expression of being; that everything that appears is transcendentally determined in a fluxional and asymmetrically ordered network of identities and differences – it should come as little surprise that Badiou holds existence to be nothing other than a transcendental degree of *self-identity*. Simply, the more a being affirms its identity-to-itself in a world – the stronger the transcendental indexing of its self-identity is – the greater degree of existence it enjoys. Existence is therefore not an ontological but rather a logical category: *to be* and *to exist* are not at all the same thing.

All of which leads us to one last crucial 'logical' result, namely that, given the concept of the minimum (after the topological requirement of an initial object), there must be such a thing as a zero-degree of self-identity, a place of *inexistence*. Or again, if, for a being *x* in a world *A*, we have **Id**(x, x) = μ, then we must conclude that *x inexists* in *A*. Which is to say that death, considered as 'inappearance' (or, more precisely, as the negative passage from appearing to inappearing), is, for Badiou, ultimately a logical phenomenon.

Chapter 2
Philosophy under condition

At the outset of this book we noted that Badiou's philosophical project is, in essence, an astoundingly rigorous attempt to think *novelty as such*, which is equally to say that his principal concerns lie with the possibility of *thought per se*: of thought as divorced from the perambulations of knowledge; of thought as that which cuts through or 'interrupts repetition' and delivers to us something *truly new*; of thought as 'the existence of a possible relation to truth, and nothing else'.[1]

It is at the same time important to point out that this extraordinarily ambitious project involves not only a wholesale rethinking of ontology and phenomenology (as we saw in the last chapter), but also a radical reconfiguring of the place of *philosophy itself*. For philosophy, as Badiou sees it, does not (and indeed, *cannot*) think for itself, but is rather entirely 'conditioned' by external factors. To be precise, philosophy is wholly conditioned by what Badiou calls 'generic procedures', namely, instances of real thought (out of which truths are constructed) that take place in the fields of art, science, love and politics. (We will consider exactly why these procedures are 'generic' in Part Three.)

The unique task of philosophy is then, according to Badiou, that of thinking the 'compossibility', or the mutual and non-contradictory co-existence, of the various (artistic, scientific, amorous and political) 'truths' which the generic procedures (or 'conditions') give rise to. Or again, philosophy's single and singular objective is that of bringing together or 're-thinking' these otherwise disparate thoughts; it is, in a word, nothing other than 'the thinking of thought'.[2] In this sense, we might say that every properly philosophical act is first and foremost an act of *reframing*: what philosophy in effect does is fabricate an empty category, which could be called 'Truth' (though its status remains wholly secondary to that of *truth* proper) under which a plurality of truths drawn from the disparate fields of art, science, politics and love might be tied together.

The conditioning of philosophy thus involves something of an inversion of the common conception of philosophical thought, wherein philosophy is brought to bear on its conditions, to contrarily contend that philosophy can only be thought – in fact, constructed from scratch – by way of its conditions.

Given philosophy's function as not the architect but rather the procuress of truth – both its collector and curator – Badiou accordingly takes a broom to the cobwebs of academic philosophy, holding that it is high time that we did away with many of its privileged sub-disciplines. 'Political philosophy' for example should be abandoned, he says, for the simple reason that philosophy itself cannot 'think' politics (which is precisely what political philosophy proposes to do), but rather can only *re*think the thought that real politics thinks. In its place he proposes a 'metapolitics', which refers only to the immediate 'consequences a philosophy is capable of drawing, both in and for itself, from real instances of politics as thought'.[3]

For similar reasons Badiou adamantly opposes traditional aesthetics, which he holds has little to add outside of establishing various rules and hierarchies of 'liking', instead putting forward his own 'inaesthetics', being an approach to art that restricts its considerations to 'the strictly intraphilosophical effects produced by the existence of some works of art'.[4] (We will consider Badiou's inaesthetic approach to art in some detail in Part Two.) Likewise, as we saw in the previous chapter, Badiou separates the properly philosophical discourse of 'metaontology' from ontology itself (which we know is nothing other than mathematics, pure and simple).

In each case the primacy of conditioning is clear: philosophy is nothing less – and, it must be said, nothing more – than the (re)thinking of the real thought that truth-procedures think.

False real copies of a false real

Let us turn now to one such condition of Badiou's philosophy – one that has only received scant critical attention to date, namely, *cinema*[5] – to help us further 'flesh out' some of the concepts we have encountered thus far.

This critical slighting of cinema is perhaps unsurprising, given that Badiou's best known musings on film appear (at least at first glance) to suggest that, far from serving to condition his philosophy, cinema is in fact of little consequence to him (a suspicion that is only compounded when we place these works alongside his more exuberant writings on poetry, theatre, music and the like). For one thing, Badiou's liberal use of terms like 'contaminated', 'impure', 'parasitic' and 'inconsistent' when describing cinema would appear less than inspiring. And that is to say nothing of his more 'excremental' metaphors, whereby cinema is associated with processes of 'purging' and 'purification', and is alternatively described as 'contaminated' and a 'waste product'.[6]

However, as with the cinema itself, appearances can be deceiving, and Badiou's philosophical engagement with cinema actually stretches back at least as far as 1957, with the publication of his first paper on film, 'La Culture Cinématographique', in the journal *Vin Nouveau*.[7] Since then, Badiou has written over thirty articles on cinema, as well as founded and regularly contributed to two separate cinema journals (*La Feuille foudre* and *L'art du cinéma*). More than this, he has appeared (in one form or another) in two of Jean-Luc Godard's films (his early work is cited in 1967's *La Chinoise*, and he appears as himself in 2010's *Film Socialisme*), and has even begun work on his own 'big feature film' on *The Life of Plato*.

What is more, when we look closely, we can discern a noticeable evolution in Badiou's thoughts on film. While previously content to define cinema as a 'bastard art', we now find him saying that 'cinema is today the only art that is cut to the measure of the world', and that, 'in publishing the final synthesis of my philosophy [...] I will try to turn philosophy toward filmic expression'.[8] And indeed, the gradual unravelling of a theory of appearing in *Logics of Worlds* and similar works arguably follows a decidedly cinematic logic, so much so that it is not unreasonable to argue that if poetry serves as the artistic paradigm for thinking the subtractive purity of presentation – as it did in *Being and Event* and other works of this period – it is in fact cinema that best illuminates the logics of appearance.

Whatever the case, Badiou holds that philosophy is obliged to engage with cinema for the simple reason that it presents us with an array of 'paradoxical relations',[9] and therefore organizes a philosophical situation.

Of the many such relations on offer in cinema, arguably the most immediate concerns those between being and appearing. Indeed, cinema, in its very nature, proposes an altogether impossible relation between artifice and reality (or between semblance and the real), and for this reason alone is generally understood by philosophers and critics alike to constitute an 'ontological art'. This is after all the 'classical' philosophical entry into the question of cinema, championed by the likes of André Bazin (among others), who famously held that 'there is ontological identity between the object and its photographic image'.[10] Like Walter Benjamin before him, Bazin premised this ontological efficacy peculiar to cinema on the basis of the relative autonomy of the photographic process, observing that while 'all the arts are based on the presence of man, only photography derives an advantage from his absence'.[11] Simply, human interference, according to Bazin, necessitates an ontological inconsistency, a definite shift away from an 'essential' re-presentation (where the object and its reproduced image are ontologically identical) toward a merely 'apparent' representation (where the image only serves to approximate the object; where the image and the object, while ontologically 'similar', fail to coincide).

Now, Badiou rejects any understanding of cinema as an ontological art on the basis of some 'essential' relation it exhibits between its own intrinsic semblance and an objective reality that remains fundamentally exterior to it. But this is not to say that Bazin's protestations regarding the inherent 'realism' of cinema must be abandoned altogether. Rather, the terms of the relationship simply need to be rearranged: cinema is not, strictly speaking, an ontological art; to the contrary, cinema is a *logical* art. Or again, film is not an *essential* art – an art of 'essences' – but rather one of *appearances* (recall that appearing, for Badiou, is one and the same as *logic*, as what appears is nothing other than a logical determination of what *is*). Meaning what is peculiar to cinema is in fact its ability to stage the complex interplay between being and being-there – between the purity of the real and the relative impurity of semblance, or between what *is* and what *appears – by way of the fiction of appearing*. Cinema is then finally not an ontological art but rather an *onto-logical* art: it is the art of appearing which dramatizes its relation with being.

So even if we can no longer suppose with Bazin any ontological identity between the object and its photographic image, this is not to say that the image fails to demonstrate any *logical* coherency. For such purely logical identity remains on the plain of appearing and thereby eschews questions of essence. As Badiou observes, 'the principle of the art of cinema lies precisely in subtly showing that it is only cinema, that its images only testify to the real to the extent that they are *manifestly* images'.[12] Which is equally to say that the cinematic image can have no ontological identity to its referent precisely because it *is image* (however, as we have just seen, this does not rule out its having a *logical* identity). Simply put, cinema does not present the real of the image; rather, it presents *images of the real*. (Or as Godard famously put it: 'not a just image; just an image'.) In subtracting the image from the visible – this being, after all, the basic operation of cinema – cinema does not cut from what *is*, but from what *is there*.

The fundamental point is, then, that the real of cinema is paradoxically internal to semblance. Meaning that cinema is at once absolutely real (in its manifest falsity) and absolutely false (in its manifest reality). Or as Badiou puts it, each and every film presents us with 'the false real copy of a false real'.[13] Yet this is precisely where cinema's virtue as an onto-logical art lies: in the very real of semblance, which is to say, in the *reality of artifice*, in its 'thinking appearance as appearance, and thus as that aspect of being which, by coming to appear, gives itself to thought as a disappointment of seeing'.[14] Plainly put, that there can be no transitivity between the thing itself and its filmic (re)appearance means that cinema truly is a *superficial art*. This assertion should not be understood as being in any way judgemental or pejorative. Rather, it simply means that cinema is an art of *surfaces*, not essences. This is in fact the very core of the paradoxical relation by which cinema figures as an onto-logical art: the art that so effectively displays the infinite wealth of being is precisely the art whose real is nothing but the desert of semblance.

Invisible prescriptions

It is not a great stretch from here to reapply Badiou's 'phenomeno-logical' apparatus (which we examined in the previous chapter) onto cinema so as to establish a complete onto-logy of cinema itself.

For one thing, in accordance with Badiou's theses on being, we can easily see that a film is, like everything, at base a multiple of multiples. Furthermore, the elements of a film are themselves just as much multiple multiplicities. A sequence for example is a consistent multiple whose elements (shots) are themselves multiples. So too a shot is a multiple made up of other multiples (frames). Further, each individual frame – those immobile segments constituting the base elements of cinema – is simply another multiple within which further multiplicities (the elements constituting the *mise-en-scène*) are carefully configured.

More than this, each film obviously constitutes an ordered set, inasmuch as it unravels in a predetermined sequence in strict accord with what Badiou calls its 'local movement', being the interminable passage from frame to frame that 'moves' the film along by continually 'subtract[ing] the image from itself'.[15] Further, this ordered set, when thought in its entirety, corresponds to what Badiou designates the film's overall 'global movement', being precisely the infinitely complex relational interplay between all the multiple multiplicities constitutive of the film. Or again: that a film forms a coherent set results from its constituting a global movement; that this set is 'ordered' stems from its exhibiting a local movement. Moreover, the term 'global' here takes on a far more definite shape, for it is clear that every filmic text, as a site of appearing, constitutes a world unto itself.

Thus our first problem: given that a film is a world (bounded, appropriately enough, by a 'global movement'), we must be able to define a transcendental proper to that world. On this point Badiou gives us two guiding examples drawn from the wider realm of art. The first lies in his consideration, in *Logics of Worlds*, of the fable of Bluebeard (in which he draws equally from Charles Perrault's original fairy tale and Paul Dukas's operatic adaptation of Maurice Maeterlinck's play, *Ariadne and Bluebeard*). Here Badiou can easily locate the transcendental of each world within the language proper to the art in question: in the arrangement of words in Perrault's tale; in the musical composition of the Maeterlinck-Dukas version.

Later in the same book, in his detailed consideration of Hubert Robert's painting *The Bathing Pool* (c.1770–80), Badiou goes into greater detail, explaining that the painting's transcendental is in effect the culmination (or the *set*) of all of the artist's successive decisions and actions (both conscious and unconscious) concerning the work: the various ways by which he has assembled the painting with regard to form, colour, light, and so on (meted out in terms of differing degrees of identities and differences), as well as his peculiar touch, his skill with the brush, the texture of his strokes, all the personal tics and flourishes that are transmitted to the canvas, and so on.

Whilst in itself a fundamentally temporal construction, this 'invisible prescription' of the artist is nonetheless finally 'recapitulated as the transcendental of a closed visibility'.[16] Badiou goes on to add that 'style', whilst not entirely equivalent to the artist's 'invisible prescription' (which would be the transcendental proper), nonetheless bears something of a family resemblance to the transcendental, so much so that we can speak of the 'transcendental field of style'.[17]

So in the final analysis we can say that the transcendental of an artwork-world rests with the paradoxical trace of the artist's invisible prescription, namely, its overall 'style', being the idiosyncratic deployment of the language (for want of a better word) proper to the world in question by the creator of this artistic world (who is, it must be noted, ultimately *excluded* from the world itself).

Which leads us to our second problem: given a film-world together with its transcendental (which we are here identifying with both its 'global movement' and its 'style', inasmuch as the former encapsulates the latter just as the latter organizes the former) we now need to investigate the upper and lower limits of its transcendental regime. That is to say, amongst its manifold objects, we should be able to locate (or at least point toward) both a maximal and a minimal object for each determinate film-world.

Needless to say, every film constitutes its own world, together with its own objects, and as such possesses its own maximal and minimal objects. That said, it would seem that the most 'sensible' place to look for the limits of a film's transcendental regime is in that most fundamental cinematic medium: *light*. After all, the very process of film projection provides a wonderful metaphor for the very operation of the transcendental (*qua* 'invisible prescription'), insofar as the projector ultimately distributes the sensible in terms of light and shadow, whilst remaining at the same time removed from (or invisible with regard to) the world itself. Indeed, can we not discern a certain touch of the cinematic in Badiou's assertion that a world's transcendental organizes 'the rational disposition of the infinite shades of a concrete world'?[18] Is not a film's transcendental precisely that which reigns over its ghostly subjects? It is, after all, a commonplace 'truth' that nothing 'appears' without light.

Assuming for the moment that cinema's transcendental regime is indeed organized around light, should we not then logically be able to discern a film's maximally apparent object as that image which shines the brightest? Were this in fact the case then the transcendental regime of a film-world would (quite literally) range from the absolutely apparent all the way through to the truly in-visible.

We might consider here the standard case of the 'Hitchcockian object', that is, the 'fascinating, captivating, bewitching, spellbinding object'[19] so central to Alfred Hitchcock's cinema, being an object which assumes a position of such importance that it literally 'overshadows' the whole of the film. Take for example the jewelled pendant that shatters Scottie's reverie in *Vertigo* (1958), or the embossed lighter in *Strangers on a Train* (1951), or better still, the glass of milk Jonnie delivers to Lina in *Suspicion* (1941) (Figure 4). Not only are these objects the ones that (literally as much as metaphorically) shine the brightest in his films – Hitchcock famously went so far as to place a light inside Jonnie's glass to ensure its absolute luminosity – but they also effectively come to determine the film itself (Judy's pendant unmasks her *as* Madeleine; the lighter ensures that Bruno and Guy's murderous pact holds; if the 'suspicious' milk is poisoned then Jonnie is indeed trying to murder his wife...).

Figure 4. Still from *Suspicion* (1941).

However, while a film's maximal object is doubtless inscribed at the level of light (*qua* image) in general, we would nevertheless be wrong to assume the equation of appearance with luminosity. For more often than not, it is in fact the central conceit of the film and its 'reverse' (or what remains, in the context of the world in question, radically alien to it) that respectively designate its maximal and minimal objects. We can easily suppose, for example, the maximal object of the standard Hollywood fare to be none other than the film's central protagonist, insofar as such films invariably revolve around (and reflect psychologically) this fundamental character. Such a film's minimal object would then be that which enters into no relation – either positive or negative – whatsoever with the protagonist; that which is essentially 'voided' from their purview.

That these figures are inscribed at the level of light does not mean that we can directly equate phenomenal luminosity with objectual (or 'transcendental') intensity. Such an equation would rely altogether too strongly on the second-order act of perception; on the notion – central to the dominant 'intentional phenomenologies' (most famously Edmund Husserl's) – of an object's existence being entirely predicated on its first being observed, according to which appearing is effectively equated with appearing-*for-something*.

It is vital to recognize that Badiou's logical phenomenology makes no such equation. To the contrary, his is an explicitly objective or 'non-phenomenal' phenomenology, one that requires 'neither reception nor constitution'.[20] An object, Badiou avers, does not need to be seen or experienced for it to exist. To the contrary, objectual appearance, in his philosophy, designates first and foremost appearing-*for-itself*: it demands no observation, nor does it require any outside approval. Or again, Badiou's doctrine of appearing is ultimately one of *pure image*, divorced from its being-perceived. In this sense, the idea of directly equating the intensity of appearance of the objects of a film-world to their relative luminosity involves an all-too subjective conception of objectivity.

That said, a film is clearly both perceptive (the image is first cut from the sensible) and something destined to be perceived (it ultimately demands an encounter with a viewer). Further, film would seem to conceive of itself – consciously or unconsciously – foremost in terms of perception (hence the abundance of theories regarding the 'gaze' in cinema).

But is perception strictly speaking *essential* to film? Here we hit upon a paradox at the very heart of cinema, whereby cinema constitutes on the one hand a fundamentally 'private spectacle'[21] – a film being of itself a 'spectatorless' enterprise, wholly separate to its public – and on the other, the greatest mass art that has ever existed.

Film as an onto-logical art

In exploring the question of the 'essential' relation of perception to cinema we can do much worse than consider the example of Samuel Beckett, whose adroitly-titled *Film* (directed by Alan Schneider in 1965) presents nothing short of an investigation into the very nature of film. What is more, it would seem that this fundamentally visual study – *Film* being silent save a curt 'shh' in the opening scene – ultimately equates the 'essence' of film with (visual) perception. Beckett himself appears to indicate this fact by prefacing *Film*'s shooting notes with Bishop Berkeley's famous proposition that 'to be is to be perceived': "*esse est percipi*".[22] Our reading of *Film* will nevertheless differ markedly from this standard Berkeleian interpretation.

So what is *Film*? Despite the grandness of its thesis, *Film* is in fact a rather straightforward work whose 'plot' (such as it is) can be summed up very easily. It concerns two characters, one 'in flight' (who is the object of the camera's gaze), and the other 'in pursuit' (who effectively *is* – for the most part – the camera's gaze). In Beckett's script these characters are accordingly designated 'O' (for 'Object') and 'E' (for 'Eye'). O spends the duration of the film attempting to evade all perception, not only by E but also by the various agents of perception around him (people, animals, pictures...). At the film's climax however, O is finally forced to encounter E, who is accordingly revealed to be none other than *himself*. Viz., O perceives E; E perceives O; *O = E*. The point being that O and E present a single, albeit 'sundered', subject.

So what *Film* would appear to be saying is that, in attempting to withdraw from all perception, O – who clearly represents a kind of 'generic' human subjectivity – finally comes up against the hard kernel of self-perception, for, as Berkeley states, being *is* being-perceived (*ipso facto*, we cannot escape perception without ceasing to be). Thus the reciprocity of perceiving-being and being-perceived – the idea that each is ontologically maintained by the other – appears at first glance to be rendered by Beckett as wholly constitutive of being itself (à la Berkeley) and, at the same time, wholly exhaustive of the 'essence' of cinema.

Now, before considering the relative merits of this by-the-numbers reading, it is worth noting that *Film* occupies a decidedly singular place both in Beckett's oeuvre as well as in Badiou's own detailed writings on him. For one thing, it represents Beckett's one and only foray into the art of cinema. Furthermore, it is one of his very few silent works. This silence further singularizes *Film*, insofar as of the four principal themes that Badiou isolates as traversing the entirety of Beckett's work – namely, the themes of 'saying', of 'being', of 'appearing', and of 'thinking' – it is the first, that is, the imperative to *speak*, that would seem to be the most immediately apparent.

Film is moreover anomalous in that it does not partake of the rupture Badiou identifies as occurring in Beckett's work in 1960 with *How It Is* (a disjunction that is better communicated by the work's original French title, *Comment c'est*, which is homonymous with the verb *commencer*, 'to begin'). As Badiou demonstrates, this text signals a decisive move beyond Beckett's previous solipsistic concerns to instead focus on 'everything that supplements being with the instantaneous surprise of an Other',[23] in the form of the chance occurrence of an *event*. *Film*, however – which was written in 1963, shot in 1964 and premiered in 1965 – in no way considers this 'new' theme. We might even go so far as to say that *Film* is adamantly anti-evental: in *Film* nothing *happens* (or again, nothing *commences*). To this end Beckett's cinematic excursus has something of an anachronistic flavour to it, a certain out-of-timeness.

In ignoring the newfound evental dimension to his work, Beckett can be seen to use *Film* to further explore some of his longer-standing obsessions, principal among these being the idea of 'thought' – as it is embodied in the 'thinking subject' (*qua* 'cogito') – as being fundamentally and ineluctably *torturous*.

This point bears some explanation. Let us begin with the obvious and note that Beckett's overall body of work – *Film* proving to be no exception – is *ascetic* to say the least. Or to put it in more recognizably Badiouian (though equally Beckettian) terms, the entirety of Beckett's thought is *directed toward the void*. Indeed, his texts are, almost invariably, fundamentally 'subtractive' processes that strip away every last layer of subjective experience in order to arrive at the brute essence of the human condition (or, as Badiou would have it, to reveal 'generic humanity'). In this sense they are, philosophically speaking, comparable to the method of enquiry adopted by René Descartes or Edmund Husserl. In fact, Badiou holds Beckett's method as being essentially the inverse of Husserl's celebrated 'phenomenological *epoché*' or 'bracketing', for while Husserl's approach consists of 'subtracting the "there is" in order to then turn towards the movement or the pure flux of that interiority which is directed at this "there is"', Beckett's basic gesture is to turn this approach on its head, such that it becomes 'a question of subtracting or suspending the subject so as to see what happens to being'.[24] Hence Beckett's insistence that *Film* not be 'realistic', but rather depict 'pure' or 'absolute' spaces, spaces of almost total abstraction.

Furthermore, we can see that 'thought' – which, we recall, represents the fourth of Beckett's principal themes (alongside 'saying', 'being' and 'appearing') – is equally the conflation of the first theme (the minimal requirement of any thought being its *enunciation*) with the third (all enunciation entailing a level of *appearing*). Yet thought is at the same time the question of what can be said about the second ('being'). That is to say, 'thought', which is constituted in appearing-saying, in keeping with Beckett's Cartesian (or Husserlian) programme, must aim at *being* itself.

Now Badiou, for his part, in his readings of Beckett, identifies this sought-after being as an 'originary silence, whose being is constituted by its enunciation, and which is the subjective condition of all announcements'.[25] Such silent-being then equally marks a 'pure point of enunciation', a point which, whilst not itself 'said' (insofar as it exhausts itself in the very act of 'saying'), nonetheless remains, if only 'minimally', on the side of being or 'what *is*'. Thus the 'torture' of the thinking or *enunciating* subject lies, on the one hand, in the fact that the very conditions of this search are, strictly speaking, '*unbearable*, charged as they are with anxiety and mortal exhaustion',[26] and on the other, in the very impossibility of its ever attaining its ascetic goal, that is, of its ever grasping the ungraspable 'originary silence' 'which is indefinitely productive of the din of words'.[27]

That said, in acknowledging the priority of the voice in Beckett's Cartesian universe, we cannot help but be struck by the disturbing *silence* of *Film*. Indeed, given what we have just seen, we would be forgiven for supposing that the absence of the voice in *Film* takes torture off the table. Yet it is clear that even in the absence of the voice, the torture of the cogito continues unabated. Indeed, *Film* is obviously concerned first and foremost with the torment associated with self-reflection (*qua* 'cogito'), insofar as its central premise is that, even after having successfully voided all extraneous perception, the 'anguish of perceivedness' nonetheless persists in what Beckett himself describes as the 'inescapability of self-perception'.[28]

Furthermore, in his one and only critical invocation of *Film*, Badiou argues that *Film*'s general schema – namely, that of object (O) and eye (E) – is ultimately insufficient, because 'the *cogito* requires not two but three terms'.[29] For according to Badiou, Beckett does not in fact regard the subject as a mere 'doubling', that is as simple self-reflection (or as simultaneously 'thought' and the *thinking of this thought*); rather, the subject is always a *tripling*. This subjective trinity, seemingly absent from *Film*, implies that there is at once: an 'enunciating subject' (a subject who speaks, and can moreover ask 'who speaks?'); a 'passive subject' (namely, the support or base matter of the speaking subject, the 'idiot body of all thinking subjectivity');[30] and a 'questioning subject' (that is, a subject who seeks to 'identify' the others, who asks what these subjects of enunciation and passivity actually *are*). Hence the self-perceiving subject (*qua cogito*) of *Film* – the simple conjunction of E and O – would seem to be fundamentally undermined.

But is it enough to maintain, as Badiou does, that the binary schema of *Film* is simply a failed instance of the cogito; less a subjective triplicity than an objective duplicity? Is it not rather that, in subtracting the enunciative dimension from the cogito so as to prioritize the object-eye relation, Beckett contrarily spotlights the very *substance* of the cogito, namely, the passive subject *qua* 'obscure matter of the one who speaks',[31] that 'idiot body' providing the support for both the subject of enunciation and the subject of the question? It seems to me that with *Film* Beckett goes that one step further, delving to the very depths of subjectivity to reveal the *brute appearance of the subject* (prior to its making-itself-apparent through the act of enunciation). Properly speaking, this 'brute appearance' constitutes, in both Badiou's and Beckett's lexicon, not a subject, but rather an *object*. What is more, this subject-object is necessarily a 'pure' object, that is, an object appearing-for-itself (recall that for Badiou the object is, in-itself, fundamentally a-subjective or pre-perceptive).

All of which leads us to conclude that *Film* – whose very title, we have said, marks it out as a treatise on the ontological character of cinema – is ultimately concerned less with questions of subjectivity than those of *objectivity*, and more specifically with what is *objectively essential to cinema*.

To this effect, regardless of Badiou's own assertions, *Film* should not at all be viewed as a failed instance of the cogito. To the contrary, it should be understood as an *exceptional* work, insofar as its subtractive aim is in fact not generic humanity (something that its ensuing unpopularity with audiences amply attests to), but rather, *generic cinema*.

To put it as simply as possible, in subtracting the realm of speech, all that remains of *Film* is image, pure and simple. This base appearance *is* its being. Indeed, this is precisely the ultimate destination of *Film*, whose concerns lie less with some (impossible) 'silent being of all speech'[32] than with the (equally impossible) invisible being of all appearing.

In failing to broach this fundamental in(di)visibility Beckett maintains the essence of cinema – its ontological halting point – as that of *appearing (in) itself*, which is equally to say that it is brute appearance that paradoxically constitutes the very being of film.

To be or not to be perceived

So as to underscore our point it is worth briefly considering two pivotal moments from *Film*: first, the opening shot of what director Alan Schneider refers to as Keaton's 'creased and reptilian'[33] eye (Figure 5); and second, the traumatic climax in which O is finally confronted with the truth of E.

To begin with, let us note that the celebrated close-up of the eye that both 'opens' and 'closes' *Film* in actual fact indicates

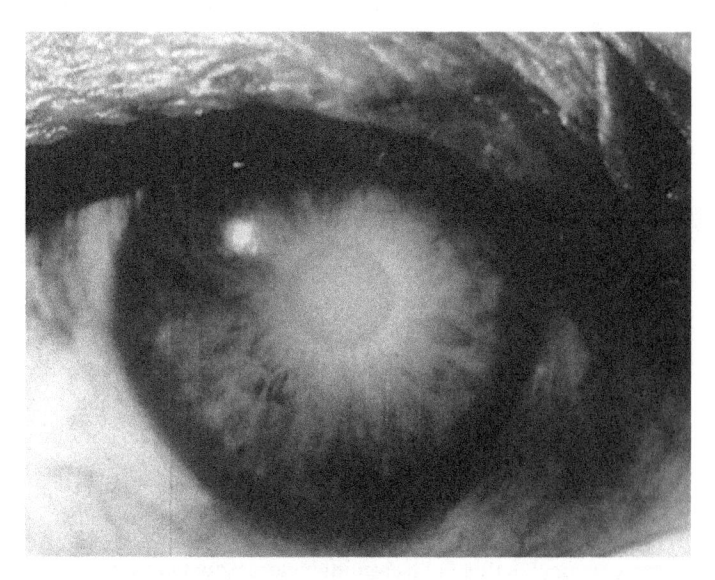

Figure 5. Still from *Film* (1965).

something far older than its 'reptilian' characterization would suggest. More than 'reptilian', this eye is, in effect, *pre-historic*. This should be taken literally: the eye in question exists prior to subjective history, prior to (and equally subsisting beyond) the story of *Film*. The eye is thus effectively *outside of* – whilst simultaneously *containing* – the very history of *Film*. Moreover, this eye is decidedly inexpressive: neither intensive nor furtive, neither searching nor sought after, the eye of *Film* is to the contrary passive, even vacant. It is, for all intents and purposes, the 'passive (eye of the) subject', what Badiou identifies as the 'obscure matter' upon which subjectivity – *history* – narrates itself.

This point has not passed by unnoticed by Beckett scholars, Sidney Feshbach for one pointing out how *Film*'s eye-image 'contains, without rhetorical inflation, its resemblance to a flower, a sun, a mandala, a cosmic map, that is, the instruments of a worldview'.[34] We might simplify this further by stating that *Film*'s eye presents a 'world-image', both in the sense that we see in the eye the image of a world, and that the eye literally *is* a world of images. It is the world of 'pure appearing' prior to appearing-for-an-other, the 'subject of passivity', the rock on which the cogito is both founded and flounders.

This pre-historic scene is moreover effectively repeated in the traumatic climax of *Film*, being the point at which O, having by this stage either removed or obscured every perceivable object – that is, every object capable of perception – and who has until now steadfastly managed to avoid directly facing E, is finally forced to perceive his tormentor, who is of course revealed as himself (i.e. as self-perception), at which point O slumps back into his chair, buries his face in his hands, and proceeds to silently rock to and fro.

How does this scene repeat the 'prehistory' of the eye of *Film*'s opening? Is this final, seemingly desperate point not simply the Berkeleian recognition of the hopelessness of escaping self-perception, of the ultimate coincidence of 'being' with 'being-perceived' (which is, *stricto sensu*, historical)?

Well, yes *and* no.

For this self-perception – the final equation whereby E = O – is, strictly speaking, *void*: O does not perceive anything outside of himself, and nothing outside of O perceives him; it is a moment of pure apperception, or more precisely, *a-perception*, the very *absence* of perception. In fact, what we see here is nothing less than a staging of appearing-*for-itself*: E appearing for O; O appearing for E; *E being O*. Thus we reencounter, at the film's terminus, the original 'subject of passivity'; the pure objective appearance (prior to subjective constitution) upon which the cogito is built.

Furthermore, inasmuch as *Film* is ultimately an exploration of the generic nature of cinema, we can see that Beckett locates the essence of film not in the subjective act of perception but rather in the 'objective' realm of *pre-perception*: plainly put, *Film* both *is* and *is about* pure appearance, appearance *qua* appearance (and not appearing-for-an-other).

So we might now ask ourselves what precisely is Beckett's take on Berkeley's formula? Does he really believe that self-perception constitutes the bedrock of being? Or, to invoke a term central to film studies: what is the status of the *desire* enacted in *Film* (a desire that doubtless circulates around escaping the 'anguish of perceivedness')?

To put it another way, is *Film*, as Gilles Deleuze argues, ultimately a question of 'transcendence' (though Deleuze would himself reject the term), of 'becoming imperceptible' (not only to others, but equally to ourselves), or of how we become one with what he calls 'Life', thereby 'attaining to a cosmic and spiritual lapping'?[35] Or is it rather a more tragic tale, according to which, as Simon Critchley (drawing on Emmanuel Levinas) has argued, while 'self-perception is what maintains us in being […] what we desire, what we crave, what we yearn for, is non-being, that is to say, the escape from being'?[36]

Or to render it in more obviously oppositional terms, is *Film*'s desire finally that of 'attaining once more the world before man, before our dawn',[37] or is it rather that of 'struggling with the irreducibility of the human world'?[38]

To put it bluntly, is *Film* a story of transcendence or of tragedy?

Our Badiouian answer is at once 'both' and 'neither'. For in subtracting the voice and exploring the purely visual (thus 'apparent') nature of cinema, *Film*, as we have seen, is finally a question of pre-subjectivity – of pure *objectivity* – which simultaneously presents us with 'the world before man' *and* the irreducible aspect of humanity. For what we bear witness to in the 'subject of passivity' is precisely the 'obscure matter' of the cogito, the 'idiot body' that is, in effect, both human *and* pre-human.

The crucial difference then lies in the relation of being to perception: whereas for Deleuze (as much as for Badiou) being precedes perception, Critchley treats the two as coextensive. We might then reformulate our question in the following manner: what is the status of *possibility* in *Film*'s avowed desire to escape apperception into what we have called *a-perception*?

Beckett's own 'scripted' answer is ambiguous at best, limited to three concise sentences: 'All extraneous perception suppressed, animal, human, divine, self-perception maintains being. Search of non-being in flight from extraneous perception breaking down in inescapability of self-perception. No truth value attaches to above, regarded as of merely structural and dramatic convenience'.[39] While Critchley prioritizes the first two points – and attempts to write off the last as an instance of typically Beckettian black humour – Deleuze contrariwise favours the third.

For our part, having already worked our way through a pre-perceptive (and, fundamentally, *non-subjective*) onto-logy, we can immediately rally to the Deleuzian interpretation, on the proviso that we understand this withdrawal from perception to be *subtractive* in nature. That is, so long as we do not conceive it as an ascension 'towards the luminous plane of immanence'[40] – which would constitute, for Badiou, an antiphilosophical solution – but rather as a descent toward the abstraction of being *qua* being, a descent that is itself necessarily thwarted, unable to pass beyond the point of its appearing.

For Deleuze, *Film*'s accomplished ascension is attested to by the symbol of the rocking chair that 'suspends us in the middle of nothingness'.[41] Our Badiouian reading on the other hand sees the rocking chair not as a symbol of the nothingness of the void but rather as the minimal gesture maintaining the fundamental (and wholly *objective*) knot tying together being and appearing: rocking to-and-fro, teetering on the edge of pre-perceptive phenomenality (recall O's eyes are now covered, effectively forever), yet unable to plunge into the icy waters of absolute abstraction.

Reapplying this logic to the thought of film itself (*qua* film), specifically with regard to the question of light, we see that this almost-abstract space – this place 'where light, always propagating itself, had no need to be revealed'[42] – is finally neither the mystical place of 'cosmic and spiritual lapping', nor the quasi-ground of pure being divorced from its appearing. Rather, it is the space of appearing *qua* appearing, of appearance-*in-itself* and *for-itself*, which is finally the properly generic space of cinema. This is in fact one of the ways we might interpret Badiou's assertion that the power of cinema is precisely that of 'thinking appearance as appearance',[43] namely, as being able to think appearance as brought to the brink of its appearing.

This in mind, we can easily return to the idea of *Film*'s investigating the nature of cinema to observe that the 'essence' of film is not in fact perceptive but rather *pre*-perceptive, being that of non-phenomenal appearance, or of 'logic' proper (further reinforcing cinema's status as an onto-logical art).

This is equally the lesson of both *Film* and film itself: even if in the end O and E (who are *the Same*) no longer exist, but rather 'ex-sist', *appearance nonetheless persists* (for cinema, as we have seen, is ultimately a superficial art, an art of surfaces). And it is precisely this pure appearance that constitutes both the essence and the power of cinema as such.

PART TWO

Event and subject

Chapter 3
The shock of the new

In 1917, working under the pseudonym 'Richard Mutt', Marcel Duchamp – the celebrated artist behind *Nude Descending a Staircase* of five years earlier – infamously attempted to enter an industrially fabricated urinal christened *Fountain* into the exhibition of the Society of Independent Artists in New York.

On the face of it, Duchamp's artistic prank was an abject failure: not only was the urinal refused entry into the exhibition, it was almost immediately lost: all that remains of the original 'work' itself is a photograph taken by Alfred Stieglitz (1917; Figure 6),

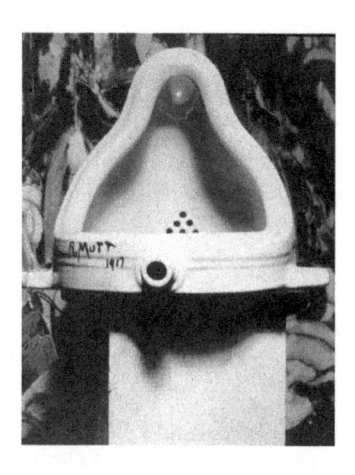

Figure 6. Marcel Duchamp, *Fountain* (1917).

though Duchamp went on to create a number of 'authentic replicas' in the 1960s.

Even so, the exhibition – or more precisely, *non-exhibition* – of *Fountain* is generally understood to be, alongside the great inventions of cubism and abstraction, one of the defining artistic events of the twentieth century. We might even go so far as to say that *Fountain*'s non-exhibition figures the paradigmatic event in the field of art; the 'event of events', if you will. For Duchamp's urinal does not simply introduce us to a new mode or form of artistic practice. Rather, 'reframed' under the name of 'readymade', it changes the very idea of art itself.

It is hard not to recognize the striking homology between the story of Duchamp's *Fountain* and Badiou's own theory of the event, which, we recall from the introduction to this book, constitutes a sudden and unpredictable break with the logic of a world (a rupture which, under the right conditions, can lead to its complete transformation). That said, we should not be misled by the terminology here: that an event *happens* does not in itself mean that the everyday world changes. Indeed, one of the main things I want to show in this chapter, by way of an analysis of Duchamp's readymade, is how the dialectic between the 'everyday' and the 'event' is in actual fact far more nuanced than it might at first appear. In particular, I want to use the example of *Fountain* not only to 'flesh out' Badiou's concept of the event, but also to explore the frequently overlooked but no less necessary imbrication of the everyday *in* the event, and as a means to counter claims that Badiou's philosophy presents a straightforward or even naïve division between conservative continuity and radical rupture.

In a nutshell, I want to demonstrate, by way of Duchamp, how, far from being a 'miraculous occurrence', the event is in fact *entirely caught up in the everyday*, being (more often than not) less a revolutionary upheaval than an 'infinitesimal subversion' by which a miniscule, even insignificant alteration in the order of things might come to exhibit profound consequences.

Appearing to disappear: the onto-logy of the event

While we have avoided engaging with it in the last two chapters, it should nonetheless be clear by now that the event is a crucial concept in Badiou's philosophy. In his own estimation, it constitutes 'the bedrock of my entire edifice',[1] and we have ourselves rather grandly called it the pivot on which his entire philosophy turns. We could even argue that, since Badiou's initial declaration that mathematics *is* ontology effectively strips philosophy of its 'highest responsibility' (namely, ontology itself), philosophy *per se* only really kicks in at the point of the event, which, as we will see, fundamentally escapes mathematical (hence ontological) thought. As such, it would seem high time that we asked ourselves exactly what it is.

Very roughly speaking, an event is nothing more (and equally nothing less) than a localized and unpredictable rupture with the order of things, involving the sudden arrival on the scene of a radically un-known element (an element whose address is, for complex reasons, immediately universal), the consequences of which might come to affect the entire situation.

Yet as we saw in the introduction to this book, an event is in equal parts rare, fleeting and fragile, and is as such quickly covered over by the powerful state of the situation. That the state must immediately quash the event is a direct – and, it should be pointed out, *unintentional* (the state being essentially a matter of structure, and not conscious intent)[2] – consequence of the latter's very novelty, which, in rupturing with the laws of the situation (namely, those of order and 'stasis'), identifies itself as *illegal* and hence a threat. As such, if an event is to have any real effect then its happening must be in some way *affirmed* by an outside party. This affirmation – together with the radical possibilities it implies – constitutes the *trace* of the vanished event (generally taking the form of a pronouncement about these new possibilities: '*x* is both conceivable and achievable'; 'it can be that *y*...'), meaning that even though the laws of the situation dictate that the event itself must disappear, it nonetheless leaves behind a mark of sorts in the form of an *evental trace*.

However, the process of affirming (or 'tracing') an event is, as we have seen, something of a tricky business. For as it turns out, we cannot *know*, strictly speaking, whether an event has occurred or not. The reasoning behind this is once again a little complicated, but essentially boils down to the fact that the 'place' in which an event takes place (namely, the evental site) is itself a point that, for structural reasons, must remain unrecognized by the state (which, we recall from Chapter 1, is what 'counts' the elements of a situation, and thereby designates which elements, legally speaking, 'count'). To this end there can be absolutely no knowledge of an event's occurrence, for the simple reason that in falling outside of the statist order – thus in falling outside of 'knowledge' *per se* (everything that is 'known' being fundamentally known *by the state*) – an event is thereby completely withdrawn or 'subtracted' from all predication.

Moreover, an event's being radically un-known means that its very happening must be, properly speaking, both *indiscernible* and *undecidable*: one can only make a 'pure' decision regarding its having taken place (the 'purity' of this decision residing in the fact that there can be no criteria upon which to base a decision concerning the occurrence of something which is radically un-known).

In sum, an event illegally 'interrupts repetition' to introduce something new in the form of a heretofore unimaginable possibility. Its radically un-known status, however, means that its occurrence is, from the point of view of the situation (or the world) in question, both indiscernible (it cannot be recognized as such) and undecidable (it cannot be proven to have – or *have not* – taken place): with regard to deciding an event's having-happened, as Badiou puts it, 'it is given to us to bet'.[3]

Yet even though we are now in possession of an adequate working theory of the event, we still do not know what it actually *is*. That is to say, it remains to be demonstrated *ontologically*. This is however once again a tricky business, not least because, as we mentioned earlier, the event fundamentally eludes mathematical thought: strictly speaking, an event *is not*, insofar as it falls on the side of 'that-which-is-not-being-*qua*-being'.[4] Moreover, between the ontological foundations of *Being and Event* and the phenomenological investigations of *Logics of Worlds*, Badiou has in fact proposed two decidedly different conceptions of the event (as well as of various other crucial event-dependent concepts: the site, the subject, etc.), and even though we are in this book privileging the presentation offered in Badiou's more recent work, there still remain substantial difficulties involved in marrying the two. Lastly, an event cannot be thought outside of its site (which provides, if only briefly, its worldly support), which itself errs on the wrong side of the laws of being and accordingly 'appears only to disappear'.[5]

As such, before we can really grasp what an event *is* we must first come to terms with its *site*. So what then is a site? Put as simply as possible (and again, prioritizing the conception put forward in *Logics of Worlds*), it is a temporary aberration of the laws of ontology. Technically, a site is an object (that is, a multiple whose elements are indexed to a world's transcendental, or a multiple that *appears* in a world) which, due to a momentary 'kink' in the ontological order, comes to count itself in the referential field of its own indexation. Or again, a site is something that 'summons its being in the appearing of its own multiple composition',[6] and as such '*makes itself* appear'.[7] All of which is to say that a site testifies to the intrusion of being *in* appearing.

Technically speaking, at the level of being, a site x proves itself paradoxical in its being a *reflexive multiple*, meaning it is an element of itself, it 'auto-belongs' (that is, $x \in x$).[8] In its counting of itself *in itself* the site thus constitutes a supernumerary term – it is, as Badiou puts it, an 'ultra-one' – and is as such, by dint of the axiom of foundation (which prohibits a set's belonging to itself), ontologically illegal. In transgressing the laws of being, the site must accordingly vanish. Lastly – and this really is key – in its giving its very being a value of existence, a site temporarily bridges the fissure separating being from being-there, which is to say it involves 'the instantaneous revelation of the void that haunts multiplicities':[9] the site convokes or 'brings forth' what is void in the situation, it presents what had been altogether unrepresented (by the state) – in short, it brings into existence what had previously failed to appear.

The *ontology* of the site thus consists of three fundamental (and, according to the laws of the situation, *fundamentally illegal*) points: it is a reflexive multiple; it is the revelation of the void; and it appears only to disappear.

A site's *logic* (that is to say, its phenomenology), on the other hand, essentially involves the distribution of the intensities of appearing around this vanished site. Of this distribution two immediate possibilities present themselves: either the intensity of existence briefly attributed to the site is maximal, in which case we are dealing with a real *singularity* (in convoking its void, the site reveals something radically new or un-known); or it is not, in which case we are merely dealing with a *fact* (the site fails to convoke the void; everything that appears is already *known*). Clearly our interest here lies with the former, which we can further divide into its strong and weak variants. Simply, while a weak singularity doubtless involves the brief (if absolute) existence of the site, only a strong singularity – that is, a singularity whose apparent *consequences* are maximal – constitutes an *event* proper.

The consequences of an event can mean one thing and one thing only, being the sudden and absolute existence of what had previously inexisted. Or to be more precise: the maximal appearance of what had formerly been the inexistent object proper to the site itself; that which constituted, ontologically speaking, the void of the situation (recall our earlier example of Dorothy's unrepresented position in Kansas in *The Wizard of Oz*). It is moreover in this precise sense – in its relating to the situation from the basis of the void alone – that an event can be said to immediately address itself *universally*, insofar as the void constitutes the 'absolute neutrality of being', which is the single 'characteristic' common to everything (given that everything *is*), and as such 'neither excludes nor constrains anyone'.[10] We will return to this crucial point in our discussion of 'genericity' in the following chapter.

Considered as a site *in extremis*, an event (or a 'strong singularity') thus essentially effects something of an existential inversion, apportioning a maximal intensity of existence to that which had previously failed to exist at all. Further, since the event-site 'appears only to disappear', this absolutely existing former inexistent represents the sole testimony to the event's having-happened, which is to say it is the very *trace* of the event, its lingering consequence. Thus Badiou can succinctly describe the event as equally 'a pure cut in becoming made by an object of the world...[and] the supplementing of appearing through the upsurge of a trace: the old inexistent which has become an intense existence'.[11]

This trace is however not logically inconsequential. Indeed, existentially speaking, every event involves a real life and death struggle. For as we know, a transcendentally ordered world demands both a maximum and a minimum, and the forfeiture of either one of these positions requires that something else must take its place. Or again, if a world's minimally existing object suddenly becomes maximally apparent, another object is required to fill the vacuum that it leaves. The logic of the event thus accedes to Picasso's famous declaration that 'every act of creation is first of all an act of destruction', on the proviso that the key terms are reversed: while creation and destruction are indeed necessary correspondents, it is creation that comes first, each and every time.

Duchamp's creative act

Returning now to Duchamp's infamous urinal, given the necessarily 'novel' nature of the event, one might immediately object to classifying *Fountain* as an event at all (let alone as the 'event of events' in the artistic field) on the grounds that Duchamp had already created numerous readymades beforehand (such as 1913's *Bicycle Wheel* and 1914's *Bottle Rack*). To do so however would be to ignore the essential *situatedness* of the event: of all of Duchamp's readymades, *Fountain* constitutes the event proper due to the simple fact that it was the first to be 'exhibited', and thus the first to appear in the situation (or the world) of art (even if this exhibition was, in truth, a *non-exhibition*). The crucial role of artistic exhibition was moreover not lost on Duchamp, who conferred an equal weight on the act of 'spectatorship', holding that 'the creative act is not performed by the artist alone; the spectator brings the work in contact with the external world by deciphering and interpreting its inner qualification and thus adds his contribution to the creative act'.[12]

In fact, as Barbara Formis has shown in her excellent essay 'Event and Ready-Made: Delayed Sabotage' (on which the following analysis draws), to categorize the readymade – or more precisely, the initial 1917 (non)exhibition of *Fountain* – as an 'event' is a fairly straightforward, even excessively neat exercise.

For one thing, like the event, the readymade emerges in the situation at a very specific point, namely, a point that is radically *unpresented*; what Badiou, in the language of *Being and Event*, calls the 'edge of the void', or the situational *site*. Furthermore, it has an 'exceptional' structure that leads to its being designated illegitimate or *illegal* by the laws that govern the situation (namely, the 'state' of the situation; in this case the artistic cognoscenti of the Society of Independent Artists). This illegality means, in turn, that its emergence in the situation is followed by its immediate prohibition or censure by the state, meaning its appearance effectively coincides with its *disappearance*. Of course, this illegitimacy and unprecedentedness equally means that there are no established criteria upon which to 'judge' the work (or alternatively, there are no coordinates by which the work might be 'positioned' and hence comprehended), meaning that, for all intents and purposes, it appears in the situation – at least initially – as absolutely *abstract*, as singularly unfathomable. Finally, and perhaps most obviously, its momentary appearance ultimately leads, through at times slow and arduous means, to a wholesale transformation of the situation out of which it arises, namely, the world of art.

Thus we already have at hand five major ways by which *Fountain*'s non-exhibition can be categorized as an event: it emerges from an eventalsite; it is illegal according to the 'laws' of the situation; it appears only to disappear; it is incomprehensible according to the logic of the state; and it results in the total transformation of the situation whence it emerged.

More than this, the 'readymade-event' – which, just to be perfectly clear, designates the *non-exhibition* of *Fountain* (as opposed to the work itself) – is paradigmatic in the field of art because its effects are felt first and foremost at an *ontological* level, that is, it involves the 'being', or the very 'essence', of art.

But we are getting ahead of ourselves.

It is first important to point out how the Society of Independent Artists – of which Duchamp was a founding member – had, in the lead up to its exhibition, taken great care to publicly establish its independence from what we might call the 'state of art'. Its slogan, after all, was 'no jury, no prizes' – a motto apparently suggested by none other than Duchamp himself[13] – while Article 2 of the *Society*'s regulations stated words to the effect that anybody who was able to cough up six dollars (the price of membership in the society) was able – indeed, *obliged* – to exhibit a work in the show.

So when Duchamp's attempt to enter his industrially fabricated urinal into the exhibition proved unsuccessful, this immediately gave the lie to both the *Society*'s 'avant-garde' credentials and, more importantly, its supposed 'independence', inasmuch as *Fountain* – or, more specifically, *Fountain*'s *rejection*, its 'illegality' in the eyes of the state – made the jury's hidden presence only too explicit. As Duchamp's friend and contemporary Louise Norton declared at the time, 'many of us had quite an exhorbitant notion of the independence of the Independents. It was a sad surprise to learn of a Board of Censors sitting upon the ambiguous question,

What is ART?'[14] Thus the work's refusal clearly contradicted the 'democratic' claim of the exhibition and revealed the *Society*'s underlying conformity with, and lack of genuine independence from, the very institutions that represent the 'state of art'.

The *Society*'s complicity with the state was only made even more explicit in the 'official' reasons given for the urinal's refusal, namely: that the object was not fabricated by the artist; and that the object was not in fact an original work at all. In other words, for an object to be accepted as a work of art in the situation 'the world of art in 1917', it had to fulfil two basic functions: first, it had to be physically *constructed* by the artist (i.e. it could not be manufactured by an external agent); and second, it had to be *unique* (that is, it must not be, *pace* Walter Benjamin, a copy of a previously existing object). Needless to say, under these conditions, the readymade could in no way have been accepted as an artwork, by the *Society* or by the state of art more broadly: as a reproduced industrial (and, in this sense, utterly *impersonal*) object – the 'artist' himself holding that one of the crucial 'features' of the readymade was 'its lack of uniqueness'[15] – *Fountain* fails miserably on all artistic counts. Were the readymade to be accepted *as* art, the very definition of art would be rendered obsolete.

And yet, as is well known, over the next half-century, *this is precisely what happened*. For far from disqualifying this non-exhibited urinal *as* art, the readymade-event comes much closer to disqualifying art *tout court*. Indeed, as Duchamp's biographer Calvin Tomkins points out, the ultimate aim of his readymades was nothing less than 'to destroy the possibility of defining art'.[16] Moreover, it is for precisely this reason that *Fountain*'s effects must be understood as being ontological in nature, insofar as they reveal something about the very 'essence' of art: not of one specific art form (such as painting or sculpture) but rather of *art as a whole*. Because what this work reveals is that all of the elements that go into making an artwork – all of those base elements which, while absolutely present (as its material substrate), nevertheless fail to be *re-presented* in the completed 'work of art' – are themselves, in a very real sense, *readymade objects*.

This is, after all, Duchamp's fundamental point: the readymade lays claim to being a work of art for a very simple reason, which is that, at an ontological level (i.e. at the level of its *being*), *all art is necessarily readymade*. Or again, there is no art that is not, in some essential way, readymade. As Duchamp explains with regard to painting:

> let's say that you use a tube of paint; you didn't make it. You bought it and used it as a readymade. Even if you mixed two vermilions together, it's still a mixing of two readymades. So man can never expect to start from scratch; he must start from ready-made things like even his own mother and father.[17]

In being 'elevated' to the level of art, the readymade thus reveals an important, if ambiguous truth about art itself, namely, that works of art require ordinary everyday objects in order to exist. Or to put it in more Badiouian terms, the readymade-event clearly demonstrates the *indiscernibility between art and non-art*, an acknowledgement that the base material of art is, first and foremost, non-artistic.

The 'evental' status of *Fountain* therefore lies foremost in the fact that it managed (metaontologically speaking) to elevate certain voided – and, fundamentally, *common* – elements from the level of *non-presentation* to that of *re-presentation*, or (on a phenomenological level) to raise that which had *inexisted* in art to a level of *maximal existence*.

Inaesthetics: art and philosophy

It is at this point that we might ask ourselves exactly what art means for Badiou. At the very beginning of this book we noted that while philosophy has an absolute need for art (being, as we have said, one of its structural conditions), art can itself easily make do without philosophy. This one-sided relationship is moreover one of the principal reasons behind Badiou's rejection of traditional aesthetics – which, we recall, he sees as solely concerned with establishing rules and hierarchies of 'taste' – in favour of an approach to art that limits its interest to the manner by which art effectively *thinks for itself*, and thus might come to affect philosophy. Briefly, he calls this approach to art 'inaesthetics', which he defines as:

> a relation of philosophy to art that, maintaining that art is itself a producer of truths, makes no claim to turn art into an object for philosophy. Against aesthetic speculation, inaesthetics describes the strictly intraphilosophical effects produced by the independent existence of some works of art.[18]

Of this definition we will suffice ourselves for the moment by noting once again that, as a philosopher, one of Badiou's foremost concerns is to examine art – or rather *particular* arts; *some* arts – as constitutive of certain universal truths, and, as such, as having something essential to offer philosophy.

We have already observed that art constitutes one of the four generic conditions of Badiou's philosophy (alongside politics, science, and love), and that philosophy, as he defines it, operates only inasmuch as it seizes these independent truths and places them in an immanent relation to one another. More than this, we know that philosophy, according to Badiou, is itself fundamentally truthless, being rather the unique discipline tasked with thinking the 'compossibility' of the various (artistic, political, amorous and scientific) truths that litter the world (and that are themselves ultimately forms of *thought*). Or again, Badiou tells us that there are truths which exist *out there*, prior to and wholly independent of philosophy, and that the latter's job is precisely that of grasping these diverse truths and 're-thinking' (or re-articulating) them in such a way that they can be brought together to cohere in a single system, which is finally what he calls a *philosophy*.

Thus the relationship between art and philosophy (or indeed between philosophy and any of its conditions) is for Badiou ultimately a 'thoughtful' one, where philosophy is charged with re-thinking the thought that art first thinks.

To come full circle, it is philosophy's structurally 'secondary' nature – its forever coming *after* truths – that leads Badiou to write off aesthetics in favour of 'inaesthetics' (which, as we've just seen, restricts itself to 'the intraphilosophical effects produced by the existence of some works of art'). In a word, it is truths that prescribe philosophy, and philosophy doesn't condescend to its conditions.

Returning then to Badiou's definition of inaesthetics, it is important to highlight how this term designates moreover the philosophical recapitulation of a relation between art and truth that is at once *singular* and *immanent*. This relationship is absolutely crucial for Badiou and as such is worth pausing to consider in some detail.

First, the relationship between art and truth is *singular* inasmuch as every artistic truth is peculiar to the art in question. So for example a truth of painting will not be found in poetry, just as music or photography are highly unlikely to produce any sculptural truths. This is in part a consequence of, on the one hand, Badiou's adamant belief that the arts constitute fundamentally closed systems (no painting is ever going to turn into music, no poem is ever going to become dance, and so on), and, on the other, the fact that every truth, while universal in address, is always the truth of a *particular situation*, and in art this situation is generally (though not necessarily) the situation of *a particular art*. Or as Badiou puts it, every artistic truth exists 'in a rigorous immanence to the art in question':[19] it is always a truth of *this* art, in *this* situation (and not another).

Parenthetically, it is at this point that some readers may be tempted to write Badiou off as just another 'high modernist'. To be sure, every so often it can appear as though he's recycling a (supposedly discredited) line of thought generally associated with the modernist project, namely, the idea that it is the exclusive commitment of each art to its proper medium that will finally allow it to lay bare its 'pure form' (or, as Badiou would have it, its 'generic truth'). Now, while Badiou may well at times be arguing something not entirely dissimilar to this, we would be far off the mark were we to reduce his thought to this kind of Greenbergian 'autonomizing' framework. While it is clear that for Badiou each art is entirely differentiated from the other arts (possessing its own form, its own possibilities, particular content and modes of expression, and so on), it is important to remember that an artistic truth is always the truth of a particular (artistic) situation, and a 'situation', so far as Badiou conceives it, is an incredibly plastic concept, which basically means *any grouping whatsoever*. So for example, while Badiou praises someone like Malevich (recall our earlier example of *White on White*) for giving us 'the generic truth of painting's singular situation',[20] he can equally celebrate someone like Duchamp, whose readymades arguably explode the very idea of medium-specificity and expose something vital in the artistic situation at large.

There is, however, another important thread to the inaesthetic knot tying together art, truth and philosophy, namely, that of *immanence*. For Badiou holds that the relationship between these terms – art, truth and philosophy – is not only singular but also immanent, insofar as every artistic work must be wholly present to the truth it fabricates. This is a slightly more delicate point, and results from Badiou's materialist conception of truths (which we will examine in detail in Part Three), the general idea being that an artistic truth (or any truth for that matter) – despite its infinite nature – is not simply the truth *of* a situation, but is moreover *itself situated*. That is to say, it takes place in a world.

To summarize brutally: Badiou holds that an artistic truth is always embodied in an identifiable 'artistic configuration', whose origins lie in a vanished event – which suddenly (and inexplicably) gives form to what was previously formless – and whose entire body is composed of the manifold artworks that belong to this configuration. Meaning that each individual artwork serves as the very fabric from which its truth is gradually woven. This 'weaving' can, in principle, of course go on forever (one can always create another work *x* exploring the consequences of artistic event *y* ...). Hence the infinity of a truth is in no way confined to a single finite work, but rather comprises an essentially infinite – or indeed, 'eternal' – sequence of work*s*.

As such, the entire 'being' of an artistic truth is located within its works, works which are fundamentally outside of artistic 'knowledge' (or outside of 'the state of art'), and as such can proceed solely by chance (this radical subtraction from knowledge being, as we have seen, precisely why they constitute a mode of *thought*). To this end, each individual work figures something like an investigation or an 'enquiry' into the truth that it actualizes, piece by painstaking piece.

So to sum up, Badiou defines an artistic truth as a material configuration that, issuing from an event, and unfolding by chance alone, comprises an (in principle) infinite complex of works. Or again, to think art as both singular and immanent to truth – that is, to think *inaesthetically* – is for Badiou one and the same as to (re)think an artistic configuration.

The disappearing act

So far our thinking about the readymade-event has focused primarily on two key features, these being its site – which we have determined to be less the exhibition itself than the unpresented 'everyday' matter underlying the artwork (or its 'base' material) – and its illegality in the eyes of the state. What we need to do now is turn our attention to the remaining 'eventural' points of *Fountain*'s non-exhibition, specifically: its appearing only to disappear; its figuring (at least initially) as an absolutely abstract work; and its ultimate transformation of the situation whence it emerged.

Regarding the first of these points (*Fountain*'s appearing-disappearing), we should note first of all that Duchamp's urinal, which is to say the *work itself*, was almost immediately lost. Discarded as garbage, or perhaps burnt or stolen: no one really knows. What *is* known is that it was absent from the Society of Independent Artists' exhibition as well as its catalogue, and was never seen again (all the various 'Fountains' housed in galleries and museums today are of course replicas). In point of fact, *Fountain* would almost certainly have been entirely forgotten were it not for the publication in *The Blind Man* – Duchamp's own review, no less – of a brief article in defence of the work entitled 'The Richard Mutt Case', which included Stieglitz's photo of the urinal, captioned 'The exhibit refused by the Independents'.[21]

In other words, after having effectively engineered *Fountain*'s refusal – for Duchamp not only entered the offending urinal into the exhibition knowing full well it would be rejected, but also sat on the jury and remained silent during its deliberations, never once revealing his identity as the nefarious 'R. Mutt' – Duchamp then went on to use his own review to denounce this very same refusal. In this way, Duchamp paradoxically *did* succeed in exhibiting his urinal in a manner of speaking, through the very act of denouncing the fact that it was not exhibited in the first place. That is to say, Duchamp's presumed authorship of 'The Richard Mutt Case' (the article itself was unsigned) essentially ensured that the non-appearance – or the *inexistence* – of *Fountain* was in fact retroactively rendered as an intense appearance, through the subsequent *exhibition of its very non-exhibition*. Or again, with the publication of *The Blind Man* piece, the readymade suddenly became intensely apparent through its very inappearance.

Thus, as with Badiou's event, the coincidence of *Fountain*'s appearing-disappearing did in fact manage to leave a definite trace, in the form of a (published) affirmation not only of its claim to artistry, but moreover of non-art's integral relation to art itself. Far from vanishing without a trace, the readymade-event contrarily performed the ultimate disappearing act, *by turning its very disappearing into an 'act'*.

Appearing-disappearing to one side, *Fountain* is not without consequence for the crucial inaesthetic concept of *singularity*. Indeed, when we think of Duchamp's readymades, perhaps the most immediate problem we run up against is that of artistic *indiscernibility*, or the paradoxical fact that such objects cannot be said to belong exclusively to either the rarefied world of 'art' – and even if they did, we cannot help but wonder: which art?[22] – or the everyday world of common, banal objects. In 'eliciting notions of aesthetic value while asserting its utter aesthetic valuelessness',[23] the readymade in fact pulls in two different directions: simultaneously art and non-art, it belongs, in an ontological sense – at the level of its very *being* – to two fundamentally opposed registers. Structurally speaking, the readymade is thus, as Formis observes, an *intervallic* object:[24] it presents itself as the interval between the event and the everyday, between art and non-art, between avant-garde novelty and the familiarity of the *ancien régime*.

Now, Duchamp himself famously theorized the intervallic structure of the readymade in terms of what he called an 'infrathin separative difference',[25] that is, an indiscernible or 'minimal difference' not unlike what we saw in Malevich's *White on White*. An object is 'infrathin', Duchamp claims, when it exhibits an 'indifferent difference',[26] or when two separate parts of its nature cannot be differentiated; when, in effect, we encounter the null 'difference of the Same'.[27]

Just as the infrathin establishes a sort of 'differential identity', blurring the line that separates two otherwise distinct things, likewise the readymade organizes an 'indifferent difference' between the work of art and the everyday object, rendering this distinction effectively indiscernible. Certainly, *Fountain* does not cease to be an industrially fabricated urinal simply because Duchamp chose it, signed it (as 'R. Mutt'), and (almost) exhibited it. And yet, at the same time, its being chosen, signed and (non)exhibited nonetheless distinguishes it from every other industrially fabricated object, and indeed from all the banal everyday objects littering the world. *Fountain* thus exhibits a peculiar double-structure: it 'presents its unity as a work of art *plus* the multiplicity of all the urinals that are similar to it'.[28] Being at the time the sole object to partake of such paradoxical double-belonging, the readymade could then be said to belong to its own unique category, namely, that of the 'readymade'. Meaning that the readymade, like the event itself, *auto-belongs*; it belongs exclusively *to itself*. Whence the simultaneous undecidability and autonomy of the readymade-event: beyond its aesthetic – or rather, *inaesthetic* – unity, it also displays its industrial multiplicity;[29] it presents itself, at one and the same time, as a single, discrete work of art, and as the universe of everyday objects.

As such, ever since the readymade-event, we could say that the world of art and the everyday world have become, at least to an extent, indiscernible, inasmuch as today any object whatsoever can be understood as having artistic *potential*, or the potential to *become* art, just as any rarefied work of art has the potential to enter into an intense relation with the everyday. What is key here is the fact that, in affirming that the very material of art is first and foremost non-artistic, the readymade-event equally points to the fact that it is art's non-artistic material that *becomes* art. Indeed, it is precisely for this reason that Badiou can hold, at one and the same time, that 'art is pure Idea',[30] and that 'the real of art comprises an ideal impurity'.[31] For, as the readymade-event so perfectly demonstrates, impurity is in fact a necessary condition – even a fundamental *law* – of art, for the simple reason that art, *real* art, always involves the formalization of what was previously formless, the radical becoming-art of what was heretofore considered non-art (or what, according to the artistic world in question, *did not previously exist*).

It is moreover precisely for this reason that all true artworks – and the readymade, as we have shown, is certainly not immune on this count – initially appear in the situation as absolutely *abstract* works, inasmuch as such art is, from the first, 'abstracted from all particularity' and at the same time 'formalizes this act of abstraction'.[32] After all, true art, in its essential (evental) *novelty*, necessarily appears as something wholly abstract to the world in which it appears (such 'abstraction' deriving, as we have said, from the fact that it falls outside the realm of available knowledges). As such, Badiou's call for a 'purification' of the arts, often misinterpreted as a naïve plea for a return to modernist sensibilities, should conversely be understood as being, on the one hand, a *destructive* gesture (one that eliminates 'apparent' impurities), and on the other, a fundamentally *creative* movement (one that formalizes or *brings into form* what was previously formless, or 'pure-ifyies' what was impure).

In fact, the case of *Fountain* perfectly illustrates the dual nature of the 'subtractive procedure' itself as simultaneously an act of *drawing under* and of *drawing forth*. While Malevich's work, for example, embodies the subtractive process primarily in terms of 'dis-appearance' (of form, of colour, of space...) – and thus as a movement toward 'purity' (understood as *medium specificity*) – Duchamp's readymades contrarily illustrate its constructive side as something that *raises from beneath* (hence 'sub-traction', i.e. 'pulling from under'). In other words, far from isolating the 'thing itself' by purging it of its inherent complications and impurities, *Fountain* contrarily establishes the impure as the basis from which all purity is constructed, exposing the infrathin minimal difference between art and its subjacent non-artistic material.

So once the readymade-event has taken place – once it has been affirmed as indeed belonging to the world of art – a certain equivalence between art and non-art is established, whereby it becomes equally possible to consider a representational object (like a work of art) *as* a presentational one (i.e. an ordinary, banal object), and *vice versa*. This exchange is perhaps most explicit in Duchamp's famous formula for the 'reciprocal readymade', in which he proposed to 'use a Rembrandt as an ironing board'.[33] In other words, the readymade-event does not simply open up a 'positive' passage from non-art to art; it also establishes a corollary passage from art to non-art. And it is of course at this precise juncture that we have located the readymade's decisive operation of indiscernibility.

That being said, obviously the readymade does not belong to both the art world and the everyday world in the same manner.

Simply, while the readymade-event demonstrates how all art emerges from non-art, this is not to say that all non-art will become art. Or again, while the everyday world is the indisputable *source* of the readymade (the urinal being, after all, not in the first instance an intentionally artistic work, but rather the product of technical industry), it is the world of art that figures its ultimate *determination* (as the readymade leads to a profound transformation of both artistic procedure and understanding).

It is, moreover, precisely this intentionality that defines both the evental nature of the readymade, and, reciprocally, the *readymade nature of the event itself*. For like the readymade, the event is itself doubly subtracted from the situation, in the sense that it is at once *drawn under* by the logic of the world in question (contravening its laws and thus appearing only to disappear) and at the same time *drawn forth* from its detritus, being entirely composed of the very material deemed to be most insignificant by the current 'world order' (so much so that it fails to appear in this world, or that, ontologically speaking, it altogether lacks state representation).

Thus the event, whilst figuring on the one hand as a sudden and absolute rupture, equally represents a kind of paradoxical continuity, whereby the order of things is in reality only minimally (or 'infinitesimally') subverted such that two elements which were, ontologically speaking, always *there*, merely come to exchange positions.

Hence the simple and immediately apparent truth declared by the readymade (a truth that extends well beyond the confines of art, reverberating equally through all the generic fields): just as all art has its roots in non-art, so too the event has its foundation – indeed, its *entire being* – in the everyday. Or again, far from being a 'miracle', the event is in truth nothing other than the spontaneous revelation of *what was there all along*. Every event, no matter how radical, exposes us to not only the *shock* but also the *schlock of the new*.

Chapter 4
The subject of art

Let us begin this chapter by casting our minds back to our earlier discussion (all the way back in Chapter 1) of the ontological 'superstructure' that is the *state*, and in particular the way in which it functions as a 'count of the count' (by which the structure of a situation itself comes to be 'counted as one'). Recall too that we noted how this statist 'reframing' of the situation was mathematically expressed through the axiom of the *power set*, which tells us that, for every set χ, there also exists a set of all the subsets of χ. So for example if we designate χ the set $\{\alpha, \beta, \gamma\}$, then the power set of χ – noted $p(\chi)$ – establishes the patently larger set $\{\alpha, \beta, \gamma, \{\alpha, \beta\}, \{\alpha, \gamma\}, \{\beta, \gamma\}, \{\alpha, \beta, \gamma\}, \varnothing\}$ (note the void or empty set $\varnothing$ is *included* in every set).

The number of subsets of a given set can then be very easily measured by the formula 2^n, where n designates the number of elements in the initial set (for example, in the above case we have 2^3 or 8). 2^n thus measures the *size* (or 'cardinality') of the power set. Let us also note that this axiom further illustrates a fundamental distinction between the originary relation of *belonging* ($\in$) and the second-order (and fundamentally *statist*) relation of *inclusion* ($\subset$).[1] For example, each of the elements of our set χ (that is, α, β and γ) clearly *belong* to (or are presented in) χ. However, we know that the elements of χ also form subsets – namely α, β, γ, $\{\alpha, \beta\}$, $\{\alpha, \gamma\}$, $\{\beta, \gamma\}$, $\{\alpha, \beta, \gamma\}$, $\varnothing$ – each of which are *included* (or *re*presented) in the initial set χ.

As we have seen, the fundamentality of the power set axiom lies in its providing the ontological schema for the protective mechanism or 'riposte to the void' that is the 'count of the count', otherwise known as the 'state of the situation' (recall that the void 'insists' within the situation by virtue of its own structuring principle, inasmuch as, in its 'operational transparency', the count fails to recognize itself as an element and thus omits being counted).[2]

Yet things get a little complicated when the situation in question is infinite. And the fact of the matter is that *every* situation is, in the last resort – and as a direct consequence of Badiou's initial decision that 'the one is not' – ontologically infinite.[3] Indeed, infinity is 'the banal reality of every situation'.[4] Certainly, when we are dealing with finite quantities the domination of the state over the situation is readily calculable: all we have to do is follow the rule 2^n. However, this is not the case when we are dealing with infinite quantifications. Suffice to say that the aforementioned indeterminate nature of the quantitative excess of the state over the situation (i.e. its *immeasurability*) results from 'Easton's theorem' – the demonstration of which lies well beyond the scope of this book – which effectively tells us that in order to designate the value of $p(\chi)$, where χ is an infinite cardinal, it is entirely consistent to simply choose *any* superior successor cardinal of χ. Or in other words, it is a fundamental law of ontology that the amount by which $p(\chi)$ exceeds χ – its *power* over χ – is essentially *unknowable*.

The ramifications of such infinite errancy on the relation of the situation to its state are both immediate and absolute: in Badiou's words, 'however exact the quantitative knowledge of a situation may be, one cannot, other than by an arbitrary decision, estimate by "how much" its state exceeds it'.[5] Put simply, the power of the state is, quite literally, incalculable.

Thus we finally come face to face with what Badiou designates the *impasse of ontology*: given an infinite (albeit measurable) situation, we cannot know – we can but *decide* – the size of its state. Between structure and metastructure (or between situational presentation and statist representation) 'a chasm opens, whose filling in depends solely upon a conceptless choice'.[6]

Which means in turn that the state – whose function, as we have seen, is precisely that of *prohibiting* the void – ironically serves to facilitate the latter's re-emergence at the very juncture between itself and the situation over which it presides: in 'killing off' the void, the state paradoxically breathes new life into it.

Fundamental to Badiou's philosophy is his contention that this crucial ontological impasse can only be overcome through recourse to an extra-mathematical anomaly, namely, an *event*. And it is to the agent of this recourse – to the figure that finally breaks this deadlock – that Badiou gives the name *subject*.

The art of the event

Before we turn our attention to Badiou's peculiar formulation of the subject, however, there is still one last thing we need to come to grips with regarding the nature of the event and its unique position in his overall philosophy, which is its *extra-ontological* status.

As we saw at the very beginning of this book, Badiou has recently come to name the tension integral to his philosophy – namely, the one that runs between being *and* event, or between knowledge *and* truth – a 'materialist dialectic'. It is on the basis of this peculiar dialectic that he opposes his own philosophical project to the contemporary 'democratic materialism' which more and more defines our epoch (prescribed as it is by master signifiers like 'relativism', 'democracy', 'capital', 'terror', etc.). In contrast to the apparent sophistry of this democratic materialism, whose principal assertion is that 'there are only bodies and languages' (or, in the more familiar formula of Ecclesiastes: 'there is nothing new under the sun'), Badiou's materialist dialectic proclaims 'there are only bodies and languages, except that there are truths'.[7] Or again: there are only worlds in which beings appear and communicate, *except that there are universal truths that can come to supplement these worlds.*

Such is Badiou's key philosophical axiom, within which we find the three principal strata comprising his thought, namely:

the ontological (the thinking of the pure multiple, or being *qua* being); the logical (the thinking of appearance, or being-in-a-world); and the subjective (the thinking of truths, or *thought* itself). Yet these three terms alone are meaningless without a fourth, being precisely the 'abolished flash'[8] that is the *event*.

We can thus discern here a clear *conditional* divide between the first three terms (ontology, logic, thought) and the fourth (event), insofar as whilst the former are each thought mathematically by virtue of three distinct *scientific* events – respectively: the Cantor-event (set theory); the Grothendieck-event (topos and category theory); and the Cohen-event (genericity and forcing) – mathematics does not, and indeed *cannot*, give us the event itself. On this point Badiou is unequivocal:

> if real ontology disposes itself as mathematics by evading the norm of the one, unless this norm is re-established at the level of the whole there must also be a point wherein the ontological (hence mathematical) field is detotalized or remains at a dead end. I have named this point the *event*.[9]

Simply, mathematics can 'think' the event only to the extent that it can think its own real *qua* impasse. Or again, mathematics only grasps the event inasmuch as it axiomatizes, or establishes *as a rule*, its own incomplete, aporetic structure (as we see, for example, in Gödel's incompleteness theorems, the axiom of foundation, the work of Easton and Cohen, etc.).

That being said, that mathematics cannot deliver us the *thought* of the event does not mean that it has nothing whatsoever to say about it. The upshot of ontological detotalization is that, while mathematics would appear to have little to say about an event's constitution (save in mathematically illegal formulas like $x \in x$), it nonetheless allows a *space* for the event to, as it were, *be* (a space which lies precisely in its aporias). In fact, ontology actually ensures such an evental space *as a rule*. We need to understand 'space' here in two ways: as an opening *for* an event (not its certitude, but its possibility, which, strictly speaking, lies in the impossibilities proper to mathematics/ontology); and as the opening *of* an event, in the sense of its material ground (what Badiou designates its *site*).

Still, it is clear that while mathematics can, in a manner of speaking, walk us *around* the event, it cannot deliver us the *thought* of its happening. To the contrary, the event, of which science must remain technically silent (and on which both the subject and the truth it carries rely absolutely), is thought exclusively under condition of *art*. Indeed, it cannot be stressed enough how it is, for Badiou, not mathematics but rather art that delivers to us the true thought of the event. For it is art and only art, Badiou says, that *supplements* ontology (at the precise point at which it is detotalized) with the thought of the event as that which *exceeds* being (or as 'that-which-is-not-being-*qua*-being'), and thereby allows us to overcome the impasse of ontology by measuring the amount by which the state exceeds its situation.

Being that it is art and art alone that thinks the event, we might even go so far as to argue that the real nexus of Badiou's materialist dialectic lies not with science but rather with the artistic condition. Or to be more precise, this dialectic hinges on the peculiarly 'subtractive' poetry of Stéphane Mallarmé, whom Badiou holds up as the exemplary 'thinker of the event-drama, in the double sense of its appearance-disappearance [...] and of its interpretation which gives it the status of an "acquisition for ever"'.[10] Thus Badiou notes immediately after introducing his materialist dialectic how in its principal assertion ('there are only bodies and languages, except that there are truths') 'one will recognize here the style of my master Mallarmé: nothing will have taken place but the place, except, on high, perhaps, a Constellation'.[11]

So the sequence of scientific events (Cantor-Grothendieck-Cohen) principally conditioning Badiou's philosophy is *supplemented* by the Mallarmé-event, exceptional in its singular, non-mathematical and axial status.

A throw of the dice

Considering exactly how this aleatory supplementation occurs is not only a fascinating exercise in itself, but also provides invaluable insight into the conditional role that art plays in his overall philosophy. To be sure, Badiou goes to great lengths in *Being and Event* in particular to demonstrate how the thought of the event is captured most perfectly in *A Throw of the Dice* (Figure 7),

C'ÉTAIT
issu stellaire

CE SERAIT
pire
non
davantage ni moins
indifféremment mais autant

Mallarmé's celebrated 1897 visual poem (even a brief glance at the formal arrangement of this work, with its idiosyncratic spacing and foregrounding of the void of the blank page, should be enough to testify to its visual nature).

In this work, Badiou tells us, the event takes the general form of a 'throw of the dice', insofar as this gesture constitutes at one and the same time both a *chance occurrence* and an *absolute*, the eponymous dice throw serving as the very emblem of radical unpredictability even as its result is one of absolute necessity, being 'the unique Number which cannot/be another'.[12] This paradoxical conjunction is moreover recapitulated on a visual level, the dispersed and seemingly chaotic arrangement of the text belying the fact that its typography has been meticulously constructed such that 'the paper intervenes each time an image, of its own accord, ceases or withdraws'.[13] *A Throw of the Dice* – both the poem *and* the act – thereby fuses chance and necessity in(to) a single paradoxical

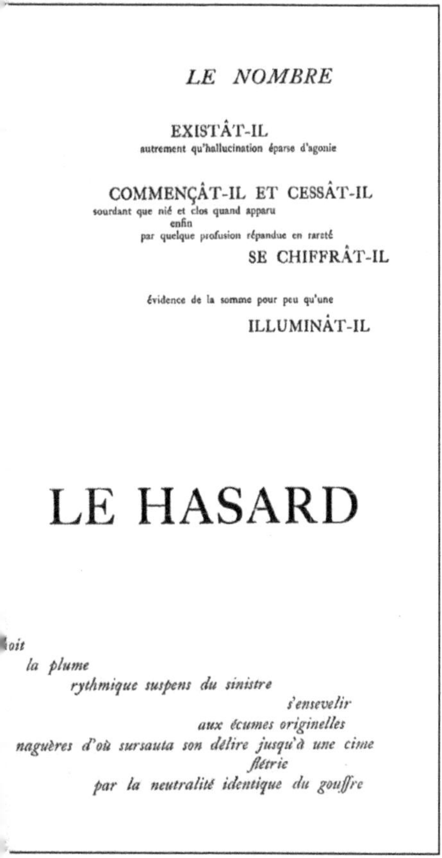
LE NOMBRE

EXISTÂT-IL
autrement qu'hallucination éparse d'agonie

COMMENÇÂT-IL ET CESSÂT-IL
sourdant que nié et clos quand apparu
enfin
par quelque profusion répandue en rareté
SE CHIFFRÂT-IL

évidence de la somme pour peu qu'une
ILLUMINÂT-IL

LE HASARD

oit
la plume
rythmique suspens du sinistre
s'ensevelir
aux écumes originelles
naguères d'où sursauta son délire jusqu'à une cime
flétrie
par la neutralité identique du gouffre

Figure 7. Detail from Stéphane Mallarmé, *A Throw of the Dice* (1897).

event, joining 'the erratic multiple of the event to the legible retroaction of the count'.[14]

Needless to say, the stakes of the poem's presenting what Badiou calls 'an absolute symbol of the event'[15] are great indeed. In providing us with the ontological thought of the event, it is then clearly not enough to simply demonstrate that it is an aleatory supplementation. Rather, the poem must also show: that it is *radically undecidable*; that it *quantifies what was otherwise unquantifiable*; that it involves the *revelation of the void*; that, as a reflexive multiple, it *appears only to disappear*; and that it nonetheless leaves a mark in the form of an *eventalt trace*.

Key here is the event's undecidable nature, as the work demonstrates that the only possible way of representing the concept of the event is in the guise of indecision itself, that is, in the very staging of its undecidability. In the poem this undecidability takes the form of an interminable indecision on the part of the dice-thrower, namely, the figure of the 'master' who casts 'from the depths of a shipwreck'[16] (that is, from a radically unpresented or 'voided' place, a place of inappearance, beneath the 'abyss' of the sea as much as the blank paper itself). Furthermore, being 'launched in eternal circumstances',[17] the master's hesitation is accordingly *absolute*, meaning we will never see him throw the dice, forever caught as he is between the decision to 'play/the game' and 'not to open the hand'.[18] This absolute hesitation is in fact crucial for the poem's presentation of the event, as either outcome would bring about its abolition: on the one hand, to 'play the game' would decide the event's presentation in (and thus *belonging to*) the situation, thereby extinguishing its eventness; while on the other, 'not to open the hand' would render the event itself null and void, meaning that 'nothing/will have taken place/but the place'.[19]

Further, Mallarmé demonstrates that even in fixing the place of the event (in the final 'number' the dice throw would present), undecidability is still not eradicated, proclaiming 'if/it was the number/it would be/chance'.[20] For were its fixity thus guaranteed, the event would either find itself swallowed whole by the regime of presentation, or simply remain void. In either case no evidence remains on which to decide the event's having-happened; its appearing having coincided with its disappearing, from the perspective of the situation, 'nothing will have taken place but the place'.

And yet, immediately after declaring this eventual non-event, there appears in the night sky – 'in a lightning flash/which imposed/ a limit on infinity'[21] – the constellation Ursa Major ('the Septentrion'), the 'essential figure of number' whose seven stars (the combined roll of a four and a three) realize 'the successive shock/in the way of stars/of a count total in formation'.[22] Thus the 'counted number' ('which cannot be another') itself emerges not only to delimit the infinite (and thus measure the immeasurable) but moreover to mark, in the face of a supposed non-event, an eventual *result*.

From the quasi-transcendence of this result – taking place as it does 'on some vacant and superior surface'[23] – we can only conclude that Mallarmé's assertion that 'nothing' has taken place 'means solely that nothing *decidable within the situation* could figure the event as such', for 'as an un-founded multiple, as self-belonging, undivided signature of itself, the event can only be indicated beyond the situation, despite it being necessary to wager that it has manifested itself therein'.[24] Or again, while it is from within the situation that we must *intervene* in the event and declare its having-happened, it is solely from outside of the situation that we can actually *know* anything of its occurrence, for the simple reason that, were it indeed knowable and hence decidable (by virtue of the given terms of a situation), it would be in no sense eventual.

The event's intrinsic undecidability – the loss of which risks its becoming a non-event – is thus compensated for on the final page of the poem, where we find that nothing has indeed taken place, 'except/ on high/perhaps/a constellation'.[25] Or in other words, the need to maintain the equivalence of gesture and non-gesture (i.e. the master's absolute hesitation concerning playing the game and keeping his hand closed) is finally remunerated 'by the supernumerary emergence of the constellation, which fixes in the sky of Ideas the event's excess-of-one'.[26] Thus the event's infinitesimal subversion of the situation, whereby it appears that nothing has taken place but the place, is finally *marked* by the (possible) appearance of a new constellation, the distant *trace* of its having-happened.

If we distil all of the above, we arrive at the essential concept of the event. To wit, the event's being a throw of the dice distinguishes it as an *aleatory supplementation* while the interminable hesitation of the dice-thrower renders this event *radically undecidable*. Moreover, in raising the master's eternal gesture from 'the depths of a shipwreck' to 'a constellation on high', it involves the *revelation of the void*, just as the sudden emergence of the 'Septentrion' that 'imposed a limit on infinity' means that it *quantifies what was otherwise unquantifiable*. And finally, its being immediately cancelled out by the situation means that it *appears only to disappear*, even while, at the same time, it *leaves a definite trace* in the form of a new constellation.

It is to this effect that Badiou holds Mallarmé's *A Throw of the Dice* to be 'the densest text there is on the limpid seriousness of a conceptual drama',[27] as it (literally) provides us with the thought of the event, marking the chance emergence of an undecidable multiple together with the possible opening of a new truth. Or as Mallarmé declares in the poem's final lines: 'All Thought emits a Throw of the Dice'.[28]

Between two impossible points

That an event 'opens' up a space for truth (or that 'all thought emits a throw of the dice') does not, however, tell us exactly how it is that we pass from one to the other. Or to put it another way, while we know that all that remains of a vanished event is its trace (which generally takes the form of a prescriptive statement concerning the new possibilities implied by the event: 'it can be that *x*...'), we nonetheless remain unsure of exactly how we get from this phantom trace to a concrete truth. Which finally brings us to the question at the heart of this chapter, namely: by what means can we move from a declaration of *possibility*, to a new (and universal) statement of *fact*?

First and most obviously, we know that a truth is always the truth of the situation whence it emerged, meaning we require some kind of procedure that individually (re)assesses the entirety of the situation in relation to the evental trace (or to the consequences of the event's having-happened). In *Being and Event* (which, as we know, is solely concerned with the level of ontology) Badiou gives the name 'fidelity' to the set of such procedures that discern all of the multiple-objects whose existence is found to depend in one way or another upon this evental trace.[29] To be 'faithful' to an event is then to 'separate out', from within a world, all of those elements that are in some way positively connected to (the trace of) this vanished event, from all of those which are not. As we will see, the infinite generic set of all of these event-dependent terms is finally what Badiou calls a *truth*.

Yet insofar as it is an *operation* (and keeping in mind that we remain here on an ontological level), a fidelity might only be evaluated in terms of its result – namely, the one-ified consequents of the event – meaning that, 'strictly speaking, fidelity *is not*'.[30] Rather, what *is* are those consistent multiples brought together *post facto* under the banner of being connected in one way or another to the eventual trace. To this effect a fidelity in fact operates on a similar level to that of the state, as in its grouping of multiples it serves to count the parts (or subsets) of the situation, meaning its ever-changing result is in the final instance situationally *included* (even if it does not *belong*). Or again, a fidelity, grasped in its real being, is nothing other than a chain of positive connections between situational (or worldly) terms and the trace of a vanished event, the 'recounting' of which is finally represented but not presented (that is, it is *included in*, but does not *belong to*, the situation).

Later in *Logics of Worlds* (with its more phenomenological concerns) Badiou introduces the term *body* to designate the finite (and fundamentally *objective*) series of these 'faithful' connections as they appear in a world. Meaning that a body, so far as Badiou defines it, is nothing other than a finite and apparent fragment of an otherwise infinite procedure, operating in 'a kind of ontological allegiance with the new appearance of an inexistent'.[31] Or again, a body is the very 'stuff' – the objective material – of a faithful procedure; it is, in a word, the concrete *appearing* of a truth.

There remains however a crucial link missing between the (vanished) event and the particular connective procedures faithful to that event, and it is to this all-important liaison that Badiou reserves the name *subject*.

Yet Badiou's subject stands in marked opposition to orthodox conceptions of subjectivity. He does not, for example, conceive of the subject as a substance (inasmuch as 'substance' would designate a situated multiple counted-as-one, while the subject – as we will see – fundamentally escapes the law of the count), nor as a void point (the void being, properly speaking, a-subjective), nor an invariable of presentation (the subject's emerging only after an event marking it out as something of a rarity). Nor for that matter is Badiou's subject a register of experience, nor category of morality, nor ideological fiction.

What the subject *is*, rather, is a formal imposition (or as Badiou puts it, a *formalism*): emerging only in the wake of an event, the subject *exceeds* the human animal as that integral structure tying together, on the one hand, the evental trace, and on the other, a new body. In knotting together a trace and a body, a subject thus effectively spans two impossible points – points with which it never actually coincides – namely, the vanished event (as opposed to its apparent trace) and the eternal 'to-come' of an infinite truth (as distinct from its present, finite body). A subject is then, in the final analysis, less a living, breathing thing, than it is a framework or formal structure that we can all, given the opportunity, enter into: it is not something we *are*, but rather something we *might become*. The subject is accordingly far more than the mere sum of our parts: it is ourselves *(re)oriented toward (an infinite) truth*. Moreover, knowing that a truth-procedure is effectively eternal, to become a subject (or to be incorporated into a truth-procedure) is, so far as Badiou is concerned, nothing less than to partake in *immortality*.

However, given that from *Logics of Worlds* onwards Badiou holds that the event itself leaves a mark (it has apparent consequences, in the form of its trace), it would at first glance appear to be incapable of offering a radically *subjective* opening, that is, a space adequate to mark the real birth of the subject. Or again, due to the fact that there is now an evental trace, the decision regarding the event's having-happened – what Badiou had, in *Being and Event*, designated a subjective *intervention* – would no longer seem to be, strictly speaking, *pure*. In part to account for the apparent loss of this radically 'subjective' dimension, Badiou introduces his theory of *points* (derived once more from topos theory), being spaces wherein the infinity of a world suddenly and ineluctably crystallizes into a binary option; where everything boils down to a 'pure choice', to a crucial 'yes' or 'no' situation, wherein only the former facilitates the truth-procedure's continuation while the latter contrarily brings about its downfall.

As with Nietzsche, a point literally 'splits the world in two', between all those objects that affirm the possibilities implied by the trace (or that are, ontologically speaking, 'faithful' to the event), and all those that do not. Points then 'test' the subject, marking as much its point of entry (its subjective 'birth' in the decision: was *x* an event or not?) as the conditions of its continuation, insofar as the course of a subject is literally dotted with points which must be held if the subject is to continue to exist. In this way the various points affirmatively held by the subject can be said to constitute the 'fibrous tissue' of the subject-in-the-world (*qua* body), designating an 'organic' path through the maze of objective worlds, worlds which – to pursue Badiou's increasingly corporeal metaphor – range from 'atonic' or pointless (worlds devoid of points, and which are accordingly 'lifeless') through to 'taught' or pointed (worlds rich in points, 'lively' worlds).

Holding each point requires moreover not only a radical decision, but also an *active* or 'efficacious' component, which Badiou, in keeping with his overall 'meta-physical' conception of the subject, designates the subject-body's *organs*. To take up once again our initial example of *The Wizard of Oz* by way of illustration, the active constituents or 'organs' of Oz's new subject – the latter being, we recall, the formal structure stretching between the eventual trace (Dorothy) and a new body (the 'militants of the Kansas event') – are obviously located in the characters of the Scarecrow, the Tin Man and the Cowardly Lion. Indeed, the very 'activation' of these figures only follows their encountering Dorothy (*qua* eventual trace) and entering into a subjective constitution (Scarecrow had been nailed to a post, Tin Man was rusted to the spot, and Cowardly Lion could do little more than hide in the forest). Incorporated into the subject, each proves to be decisive for its continuation, rescuing Dorothy when she is imprisoned by the Wicked Witch (Cowardly Lion sneaks into the castle in which she is held, Tin Man cuts down the door imprisoning her, and Scarecrow traps the guards under a chandelier before inadvertently revealing the Wicked Witch's watery weakness).

In explicating the link between the event and its ensuing truth, Badiou thus presents a distinctly corporeal image of a decidedly inhuman subject, whose body is constituted by points (together with their efficacious organs) which form a kind of fibre spanning the course of – or drafting a map of – the new world.

The artistic imperative

We saw in the previous chapter how Badiou's peculiar approach to art – what he calls 'inaesthetics' – marks the philosophical recapitulation of a relation between art and truth that is at once singular (the artistic truth belongs exclusively to the art in question) and immanent (the artistic works are wholly present to the truths they fabricate).

In thinking this relation, however, a complication immediately arises concerning the distinction between *finitude*, on the one hand, and *infinitude*, on the other. For while a truth is, as we know, an infinite multiplicity whose origin lies in a since-vanished event, an artwork is, to the contrary, most assuredly *finite*. In fact, Badiou even goes so far as to suggest that 'art is the only finite thing that exists'![32] So to think the relation between art and truth, we must be able to somehow think the infinite as immanent to – or as being in some way contained within – finitude. Moreover, given that an artistic event is obviously going to be related, at least to some degree, to a novel artwork, we must also be able to think the relation between a fundamentally *present* work and a necessarily *past* (or vanished) event.

To think 'inaesthetically' is then to think a triply paradoxical relationship, being the one that exists between an artwork (which is both *finite* and *present*), an event (which, whilst *finite*, takes place or 'ex-sists' in the *past*), and a truth (which, as *infinite*, only comes to be in the *future*).

Making sense of these paradoxical relations (between finitude and infinitude; between past, present and future) is no small task. Probably the best place to start is by asking ourselves the question that we have steadfastly managed to avoid tackling thus far, namely, the question of *what exactly constitutes an artistic event*. For even though we have discussed the event itself in considerable detail, we have until this point employed art exclusively as a means to examine the nature of the event *qua* event (as for example we did with both Duchamp and Mallarmé).

Through all of this we have not really considered what an event *in art* actually is.

To isolate an artistic event, however, we first need to locate, in a specific artistic situation, a *site*. Formally speaking, this is in fact a rather simple exercise (even if it is extraordinarily difficult in practice). For such a site is necessarily going to exist at the very edge of what is perceived, in the artistic world in question, as being *devoid of form*: lying, as it does, on the edge of the void, the site will be the closest we can come to – without crossing over into – radical formlessness. Ergo, as with ontology itself, the artistic site is situated around a *formal impasse.*

An event in art – which, as we know, involves the maximal appearance of what had previously remained 'void' in the situation – will then involve the 'accession to form' of what had up to this point been radically formless. Suddenly and disturbingly, a new artistic work (or group of works) arrives on the scene and displaces the frontier between sensible form and insensible formlessness. Suffice to recall here our example of the readymade-event: that Duchamp's urinal displaces the distinction between art and non-art (and thereby establishes impurity as the basis from which all purity is constructed) clearly marks it as an event in the history of art. Technically speaking, an artistic event is thus what crystallizes or 'formalizes' what was previously 'inform' (as, in more general terms, an event brings into existence something that previously 'inexisted').

It is moreover for precisely this reason that Badiou holds an artistic truth-procedure to be, in essence, something that gives form to what had previously remained formless (or 'inform'). The imperative of art is thus that of 'inscribing the inexistent'; of making 'sensible' or bringing into sense (where 'sense' is understood in terms of both appearance and knowledge) that which fails to make sense in the world to which the art in question belongs. Or in other words, real art is nothing other than novel formalization at its purest level.

And yet, while a work (or more precisely, the initial and decisive *presentation* of this work; its disruptive emergence in the situation) *can be* an event, it can never be a truth. To the contrary, an artistic truth is nothing other than an ongoing artistic procedure. More precisely, a truth of art is embodied in what we earlier referred to as an identifiable artistic configuration, the origin of which lies in a vanished event (being the initial appearance of works that formalize what was previously formless), and whose material body is composed of the manifold artworks that make up this configuration (each individual artwork serving, as we have said, as the fabric from which its truth is gradually woven). An artistic body is thus the set of works constituted in the wake of an event, works that 'treat, point by point, the consequences of the new capacity to inform the sensible'.[33] Hence, as we have said, the infinity of a truth is in no way confined to a single *finite* work, but rather comprises a virtually *infinite sequence of works*.

More than this – and once again in keeping with Duchamp's fundamental contention that 'the onlooker is as important as the artist' – the spectator him- or herself can equally be incorporated into an artistic body. For if they are to comprehend these novel works – works which, as we know, initially appear as abstract due to the fact that they cannot be adequately placed within the existing artistic regime (*qua* state of art) – he or she must transform their very subjectivity, their *individuality*, in order to make sense of the work's novel formations.

One important consequence of all of this is that we must reject the classical conception of the artwork's creator as constituting its true subject, or as being the ultimate arbiter of its meaning. For if we follow Badiou's logic, we must contrarily concede that an artistic subject can in no way be the artist (whose invisible prescription, we saw in Chapter 2, constitutes the work's transcendental, yet who is finally excluded from the work itself), but rather must be the ever-expanding set of works unfolding in a broader artistic truth-procedure. As Duchamp himself keenly observed, the artist ultimately means nothing:

> As far as art history is concerned, we know that in spite of what the artist said or did, something stayed on that was completely independent of what the artist desired; it was grabbed by society, which made it its own. The artist doesn't count. *He does not count.*[34]

The entire 'being' of an artistic subject – its material *body* – is thus located, on the one hand, in the various works that make up this new artistic configuration (and that constitute so many 'enquiries' into the truth that it actualizes, piece by piece), and on the other, in the various individuals who are incorporated into this truth along the way insofar as they reconfigure their way of relating to this art (and in this way contribute to its gradual *discernment*).

In sum, an *artistic event* involves the initial appearance in the situation of a novel work or group of works that displace the frontier between sensible form and insensible formlessness by formalizing what had previously been 'inform' (or devoid of form) in the situation. Such an event may invoke a new artistic *subject*, whose *body* is composed of the manifold artworks and figures that experiment with the implications of this new formal possibility, and in so doing constitutes a new identifiable artistic configuration. This new subject accordingly ties together the *trace* of the vanished event (for even if the work itself endures, the same cannot be said of its initial disruptive appearance) with its ultimate *truth*, which will be the final recollection of all of these works into an infinite generic set.

Outside of rethinking the thought that such configurations produce, the role of philosophy is accordingly that of demonstrating how they fall under the category of *truth*. Countless such configurations are scattered throughout the history of art: in Greek tragedy, from Aeschylus to Euripides; in the European novel from Cervantes to Joyce, etc. That we can identify both a beginning and an end to these sequences does not, however, negate their infinite, eternal nature. The fact that a configuration may reach a point of *saturation* – that is, the point at which the resources of the situation have dried up to the extent that its novel explorations cease to be properly inventive (or are no longer artistically 'interesting') – need not spell a truth's *finitude*. To the contrary, a truth, so far as Badiou conceives it, is at once effectively *eternal* (it is available for all time: even if it disappears in one world, it can always reappear in another) and intrinsically *infinite*, being that which 'ignores every internal maximum, every apex, and every peroration'.[35]

Consider for example the great musical truth-procedure known as Serialism (a configuration that amply testifies to a truth's eternal nature, given that it names to this day our truly 'contemporary music'). This procedure is initiated by the Schönberg-event that 'breaks the history of music in two'[36] through the discovery of the (previously unimaginable) possibility of the establishment of a musical world which is not subordinated to classical tonality. Once vanished, this event is constrained only by its trace, which is basically an affirmative statement regarding the possibilities it implied, of the kind: 'an organization of sounds may exist which is capable of defining a musical universe on a basis which is entirely subtracted from classical tonality'.[37]

The subject of the subsequent musical truth is accordingly the concrete 'becoming' of dodecaphonic music, whose *body* is located less in the composers and musicians themselves than in the various works written and performed that experiment with the possibilities implied by the evental trace, and in so doing gradually construct a new musical world on its affirmative basis. If this sequence (which, along with Arnold Schönberg, was principally carried by the proper names Alban Berg and Anton Webern) eventually found itself saturated by the close of the 1970s, this simply reflects the fact that 'every subject, albeit internally infinite, constitutes a sequence whose temporal limits can be fixed after the fact'.[38] Or again, whilst its *possibilities* remain infinite, its 'corporeal capacities' – that is, its subjective body, together with all those resources presented in the situation that might still inscribe themselves in the dimension of the work – finally became too restricted.

So even though a truth-procedure itself is both essentially eternal and intrinsically infinite, once its 'corporeal capacities' have dried up 'an infinite subject reaches its *finition*'.[39] Thus we see that every truth is at once eternal *and* provisional, immortal *and* mortal, transcendent *and* mundane.

Genericity and the fundamental law

We have already noted how a truth is, ontologically speaking, the infinite generic set of all of a world's event-dependent terms. Or again, a truth is the 'complete' – or more precisely, 'quasi-complete' (infinite sets being themselves necessarily 'incomplete') – set of all of the productions of a faithfully subjectivated body.

That a truth is *infinite* means not only that it is (in the language of Cantor) a 'transfinite set', but also that its procedure entails a (for all intents and purposes) endless sequence of affirmative connections to an evental trace.

That it is *generic*, on the other hand, means that it is absolutely a-particular or 'indiscernible' with regard to the situation of which it is a subset, due to the fact that it is composed entirely of enquiries which themselves manage to 'avoid' every property formulable in the language of the situation.[40] A truth's genericity thus means that it remains fundamentally '*indiscernible and unclassifiable* for knowledge':[41] not only can the state not spot a truth for what it is, but it cannot know anything about it either.

The evental origin of a truth moreover precludes (as we have seen) its being mathematically explicable (insofar as the event, as 'that-which-is-not-being-*qua*-being', ontologically ex-sists). However, even though mathematics has, strictly speaking, nothing to say about the concrete production of a truth, it can nevertheless – through recourse to Paul Cohen's fabulously difficult generic set theory (the complexities of which are in irremediable excess of the concerns of this book) – delineate its ontological *form*. This is an intricate and important point that we will return to in the following chapter. For the moment, we simply need to note that if a truth is, ontologically speaking, an infinite and 'excrescent' collection – meaning its terms are *represented* but not *presented* (i.e. ⊂ but ∉) – of all those affirmatively investigated terms in the situation, then this subset (*qua* faithful subject-body) qualifies as 'generic' if and only if it evades each and every criteria of discernment that is available in the situation (and is to this effect, strictly speaking, 'unknowable').

The question remains however as to how exactly this is the case. In answering this we first need to note that, being counted (included) by the state, yet having no discernible or expressible property, the entire being of a truth resides in its being a *subset*, that is, in the fact that it is composed of multiples that are themselves presented in the situation. Such an indiscernible *inclusion* can then have no 'property' other than that of referring to *belonging*. Moreover, as this property – which is nothing short of *being*, pure and simple – is obviously shared by each and every term of the situation (inasmuch as they all *are*), the indiscernible subset solely possesses the properties of *any set whatsoever*: of the generic subset 'all one can say is that its elements *are*'.[42] It is in fact in this precise sense that such a generic set presents the properly *universal* truth of the situation, since the indiscernible subset grasps and exhibits 'the very being of what belongs insofar as it belongs'.[43]

And yet, one might object, if all that one can say of such a generic set is that its elements *are*, surely this renders a truth impotent? What, after all, can such a truth actually *do*? As an excrescent multiple (⊂ but ∉), the 'true' subset does not even belong to the situation. Furthermore, by virtue of its genericity, it remains radically 'subtracted' from knowledge, meaning that it does not actually *say anything* (at least, nothing comprehensible). What then becomes of the *affective* aspect of truth, and where exactly does this leave the garden-variety militant?

For a truth to have any real effect (or for it to be *presented* as such) its belonging must be in some sense *forced* upon the world, thereby establishing a *new* world in which it *will* be discernible (which is to say 'knowable'). Only in this way might a truth truly have anything to say. Such 'forcing' – the mathematics of which is, once again, provided by Cohen – constitutes what Badiou calls 'the fundamental law of the subject'. While the precise mechanics of forcing are somewhat complicated (in fact, they constitute some of the most difficult sections of *Being and Event*), in essence they demonstrate how an indiscernible subset of a situation (i.e. a generic multiple) can come to be discernible, specifically through 'forcing' certain otherwise undecidable statements about this multiple to be recognized as either 'true' (or more precisely, 'veridical') or 'false'. Or in other words, Cohen's work on forcing demonstrates how it is in fact entirely possible 'to determine under what conditions such or such a statement is veridical in the generic extension obtained by the addition of an indiscernible part of the situation'.[44]

To explain: in order to render the indiscernible subset 'known' – to force it, as it were, to *be* (or to produce 'new knowledge') – it is clear that the language of the situation must itself undergo radical transformation, so that it can be accommodated therein. It is to this effect that the subject tasks itself with re-signifying names and words that are already present in the established language of the situation, even if, from the latter's point of view, these new significations do not yet make any sense (due to the fact that their referents remain suspended from the infinite becoming of a truth). Such re-nominations ultimately constitute a new 'subject-language' which, whilst certainly recognizable, will nonetheless initially appear to the outside observer as both arbitrary and contentless (by virtue, as we've said, of its suspension from the 'to-come' of a truth). Yet – and herein lies the fundamental wager of the subject – they *will be* comprehensible once the *new* situation (namely, the 'generic extension' of the old situation) has been established. Operating in accordance with the logic of the future anterior, forcing thus 'names a point in a situation where the situation's inconsistency will have been exposed',[45] or where its truth *will have been made clear.*

A true subject – a subject of truth – thereby literally forces the situation 'to dispose itself such that [its] truth – at the outset anonymously counted as one by the state alone – be finally recognized as a term'.[46] In this manner subjects really do change the world, 'not by what they discern, but by what they indiscern therein'.[47]

Thus we finally arrive at a point where a truly nuanced definition of subjectivity can be given. First, we know that the subject is an absolutely *anterior* function, inasmuch as it (might) come about only after the chance occurrence of an event. Second, despite its formal nature, the subject has both a dynamic and an extensive dimension (the former lying, as we have seen, with the evental trace; the latter in its corporality, namely, its body and efficacious organs). Further, by way of its 'fundamental law' – that is the forcing of indiscernible terms – the subject, militating around the trace of the vanished event, precisely locates itself 'at the intersection, via its language, of knowledge and truth':[48] oriented towards (yet forever separated from) truth by an infinite series of haphazard enquires, the subject works to trace out, in the world in question, 'the becoming multiple of the true'.[49]

In a nutshell, the subject represents the 'synthetic' function of Badiou's materialist dialectic, tying together being *and* event, knowledge *and* truth: just as all that *is* is woven from the void, so too the subject is woven from a truth (which draws its power from the void), through which everything that already *is*, is subjectively rewritten.

PART THREE

Truth and ethics

Chapter 5

From here to eternity

In beginning this third and final section on 'Truth and Ethics', we could do much worse than to ask ourselves one of the oldest questions in the book: *what is philosophy?*

As ever, it is easiest to approach this question by first considering what it is not.

For one thing, philosophy is clearly not a process of invention. As we have seen, philosophy does not even so much as *think* for itself (insofar as 'thought' is the sole domain of the generic conditions). Nor, for that matter, is it an act of intervention (which is contrarily the exclusive preserve of the subject). Neither is philosophy an activity of passive contemplation (despite the common caricature of the impotently cerebral philosopher), nor the instrument of a comprehensive 'world view' (that philosophy's sole quarry is truth necessitates an indifference to broad sections of the world). Likewise, philosophy is not an act of conversation (truth being precisely that which cuts a swathe through the field of opinions), nor one of conversion (which contrarily occurs during the course of a truth-procedure).

To the contrary, philosophy is more akin to a process of *recuperation*: not only does philosophy seize, combine and systematize (or 'compossibilize') thoughts that are, in truth, fundamentally alien to it, but it also reappropriates concepts that already exist – and may even still have major currency – in the situation as it stands (much in the manner that a truth-procedure generates a new subject-language out of terms that already exist in the situation).

Indeed, real philosophy, broadly speaking, can be understood as a systematic process of defamiliarization and resignification. Badiou's own work is a case in point. Consider the key concepts that make up the various sections of this very book: being and appearing, event and subject, and now, truth and ethics. All of these terms are familiar philosophical concepts that have been radically reconfigured, their significations so altered that in some cases they bear scant resemblance to their original meanings.

Take for example the elementary concept of the 'subject'. We tend to naïvely conceive of the subject along the lines of an autonomous and stable entity – the 'core' of the self – fully endowed with consciousness, and representing the 'authentic' source of action and meaning. But what has philosophy 'done' to our understanding of this concept? In the last century alone the subject has undergone a massive transformation. Sigmund Freud, for example, showed how it is riven by unconscious desires, while Lacan theorized it as a void point, the 'empty waste' of the cogito. Louis Althusser, for his part, argued that it constituted an ideological fiction, while phenomenologists like Maurice Merleau-Ponty designated it a register of pure experience. Michel Foucault contended the subject was produced by discourse, while Levinas understood it as a category of morality. The list could easily go on. Accordingly, by the time we reach Badiou, the 'subject' (together with its meta-physical sub-concepts: 'body', 'organs', and the like) bears little resemblance to our original conception. The concept has been transformed into something radically new.

We could easily list further examples. 'Being', Badiou says, is pure multiplicity, the thought of which is provided by mathematics and mathematics alone. 'Appearing' is a logical category. 'Truth' is an infinite generic multiplicity. And so on.

Radical resignifications such as these serve to defamiliarize existing concepts at the same time as they create new and complex relationships with each other. Contrast for example Badiou's theory of the event with Deleuze's (as he himself does in a crucial section of *Logics of Worlds*) and you will encounter two utterly opposed conceptions. Or consider Badiou's understanding of ethics (as we will in the following chapter) in light of the celebrated work of Levinas, and you will find little in the way of common ground.

The point being that while philosophy *transforms* concepts, it does not, strictly speaking, invent them. Rather, they are invented outside of philosophy, through the course of generic procedures. Properly speaking, concepts – or Ideas, to give them their classical philosophical name – belong to the domain of truth. As such, while philosophy can be said to reconceptualize or 'reframe' concepts (or 'rethink thought'), we need to keep in mind that this is ultimately a second-order activity. Rather, as we have said, philosophy's real role is that of seizing, combining and systematizing concepts (Ideas) that are first drawn from elsewhere, from specific instances of art, of politics, of science and of love.

And it really is the *systematic* nature of this re-conceptualization that makes a philosophy. This is, incidentally, the principal reason as to why we have sought to reproduce in this book the systematic structure of Badiou's overall philosophy – against, on many occasions, its actual temporal development (which has been far from linear) – beginning first with his reconceptualization of being and appearing before broaching the transformative question of the event and the subjects and truths that might follow.

The story so far

Thinking of philosophy's systematic nature, now would seem as good a time as any to present a brief summary of our journey up to this point.

In Part One we noted that Badiou's 'mature' philosophy begins with his declaration that 'mathematics *is* ontology'. Or more precisely: ZFC set theory (which is the pre-eminent foundational system for mathematics) gives us the science of being *qua* being, or being subtracted from all of its particular qualities and attributes. The argument behind this was, it must be said, rather complicated, but essentially boiled down to the fact that being itself – *pure being* – is, according to Badiou, nothing other than 'inconsistent' or 'multiple multiplicity', and such multiplicity is precisely what ZFC set theory spends its time thinking. Moreover, set theory also thinks both the enframing of inconsistent multiplicity (its presentation or 'one-ification'), as well as its subsequent reframing (or 're-presentation'). Basically, set theory *is* ontology because it provides us with the entire discourse on being, from the void of inconsistent multiplicity all the way up to structured situations and the states that legislate over them.

Yet as we saw, establishing a coherent ontology is alone not enough; situations must be conceived simultaneously in their *being* (i.e. as pure/inconsistent multiplicity) as well as their *appearing*, namely, as the effect of a transcendental legislation. Yet the set-theoretic resources of *Being and Event* – resources that are constrained (through the axiom of extensionality) to recognize only absolute identity and difference – are clearly incapable of providing such a relational thought. Thus the parallel claim governing *Being and Event*'s belated sequel, *Logics of Worlds*, that *logic* (or more precisely, *category-theoretic logic*) *is appearing*. For it is in this work that Badiou fleshes out a logical phenomenology to complement his mathematical ontology, thereby providing a complete onto-logical theory of *being-there*.

In Part Two we turned our attention to the 'radical' side of Badiou's philosophy, focusing in particular on his transgressive and transformative concepts of the *event* and the *subject* and their relation (or rather, *non-relation*) to the orders of being and appearing.

We began by defining the event as a localized and unpredictable rupture with these distributive orders, whereby a previously unknown and inconsequential object – an object that, whilst assuredly (ontologically) *part* of the world in question, is so alien to its prevailing logic that it can be said to 'inexist' within it – is suddenly exposed as *maximally consequential* and elevated to the level of an existential absolute.

That said, for all its power and promise, we saw how an event is at the same time rare, fragile and fleeting: prohibited by the laws of ontology – the very same laws that (paradoxically) guarantee a space for its 'coming-to-be' – the evental rupture poses a direct threat to statist order, and as such is cancelled out almost as soon as it appears. Doubly subtracted from the situation (being simultaneously 'drawn out' of its waste material, and 'drawn under' by its logic), the event may well bear the appearance of a miracle, but its structure is nevertheless as mundane as the world in which it takes place.

Once vanished, only a trace of the event remains, which simply points to the possibilities opened up by its having-happened. This trace, however, can mark the birth of a new subject, which, as we saw, is itself a formal structure tying together, on the one hand, the evental trace, and on the other, all the objects of the world that are found to be in some way 'faithfully' connected to its particular affirmation(s). Taken together, these objects constitute the subject's growing 'body' as it is gradually constructed through a long and difficult process of experimentations and investigations into the relation of the evental trace to the world in question.

At the far end of this procedure – at its *terminus* – lies a new universal *truth*, that is phenomenally borne out by the new body (which, we saw, is what bears the 'subjective appearance' of a truth, marking its concrete appearing-in-a-world), while being ontologically conceived of in the form of an infinite generic set whose belonging must be forced upon the situation by the subject, in a process that Badiou designates its 'fundamental law'.

And yet we also saw that these last two crucial elements of Badiou's philosophy – event and subject – are not in fact questions of being or appearing (thus ontology or logic), but are rather of an altogether different order. For even though events and their (possibly) ensuing subjects can certainly be *formalized*, they nonetheless remain fundamentally *other* to ontology. Or again (recalling our initial division between knowledge and thought), while these concepts may be mathematically *known*, they cannot be mathematically *thought*. To the contrary, we saw that the event, on which the subject relies for its very being, is contrarily thought by art and art alone (even if mathematics can, in a sense, grasp something of the event by thinking its own impasse).

All of which gives us pause to think a little more about the role of conditioning in Badiou's philosophy. For as we saw in Part One, Badiou holds that philosophy, having no real thought of its own, only exists by virtue of its conditions, which he identifies as being limited to the 'generic' fields of art, science, politics and love. In thinking the compossibility of the thoughts that these disparate fields think, philosophy itself must be understood as being, from the very first, an act of 'reframing', whereby the various concepts or Ideas already available in the situation are gathered up and placed – perhaps against their will – into strange and unfamiliar relations with each other.

While we have spent a good deal of time thinking about art in this respect (its philosophical recapitulation as 'inaesthetics'; its thinking of the event at the very limits of scientific knowledge), it would seem that we haven't really considered the other conditions in much detail at all. What then of science, politics and love? How do they fit into Badiou's broader philosophy?

Beyond art

While it may not have been altogether obvious at the time, the fact is that we have already thought quite a bit about science and truth. In Part One for example we paid close attention to two different scientific truth-procedures, namely, the discourses of set theory and category theory (in our explications of being and appearing respectively). To single out only the first of these, 'set theory' (and moreover ZFC) in fact designates a very specific truth-procedure in the history of science. Indeed, it is this very procedure that conditions the fundamental philosophical idea that 'mathematics is ontology'. Its founding event is Cantor's conceptualization and consequent (if unintended) laicization of the *infinite* – a concept that had been crucial throughout the history of mathematical analysis but had nevertheless remained vague and unformulated – and its body is constituted not only by Cantor's on-going work on sets and infinite quantifications, but also through its subsequent axiomatization by Zermelo, Fraenkel and others.

What is more, we can observe a certain formal affinity between science and art, inasmuch as they both involve a kind of novel formalization: whereas an artistic truth formalizes what had previously been formless (or brings the 'inform' into form), we might say that a scientific truth 'literalizes the illiterate'. For science, so far as Badiou is concerned, is ultimately a question of *submission to the (mathematical) letter*. To explain: if 'science' can be understood in general terms as 'the rational theory of those phenomena in the world which do not depend upon the conscious activity of man',[1] it follows that mathematics constitutes a necessary dimension of *all* scientific discourse, as it is in each and every case the formal dimension of the former that supports the latter's more abstract and general strata. A 'scientific world' is then, in essence, the exposition of what *is* (as much as what *is there*) not in its direct givenness, but rather in its underlying schema, or the discerned laws and formulas of being and appearing (or of 'being-there'). Accordingly, every scientific world exhibits a definite frontier between the *mathematized* – namely, what has already submitted itself to the power of the (mathematical) letter – and that which resists mathematization (much in the manner that an artistic world exhibits a fundamental division between form and formlessness).

A scientific event thus involves the sudden displacement of this frontier, a displacement that is detained in a trace which marks the fact that an otherwise 'abstract disposition of the world [...] emerges into symbolic transparency'.[2] The post-eventful scientific body then constitutes itself as the collection of laws, theorems, principles and so forth relating to this new disposition, which fall under the broad heading of 'results', and which serve to produce a new truth in the form of a 'new scientific theory'.

Likewise, we have also thought a little about politics, in our initial example of *The Wizard of Oz*. Here we noted, in essence, that political worlds are defined by their exhibiting a radical split between presentation and representation, or between 'the people' (broadly considered as a single, presented multiple) and the superpower of the State. Politics proper then begins only after an event not only exposes the void of the situation – this being precisely what had altogether failed to be 'legally' presented (or 'inappears') in the world in question (in our own earlier example: Dorothy herself) – but moreover succeeds in 'fixing' the superpower of the State. This initial eventual 'measuring' (*qua* 'political prescription') is thereafter sustained by a sequence of 'organized collective action, following certain principles…[which aim] to develop in reality the consequences of a new possibility repressed by the dominant state of affairs'.[3] Thus a new political body is constructed (under the injunction of the trace of an event) in the form of an *organization*, which ultimately serves to produce a new truth embodied in an identifiable 'political sequence'.

So far, so good.

But what about love? What exactly is love, philosophically speaking?

First and most obviously, like every generic procedure, love is, according to Badiou, wholly entwined with the register of truth, and as such exceeds sentimentality as much as sexuality. In point of fact, Badiou's take on love essentially departs from the infamous Lacanian thesis that 'there is no sexual relation'.[4] This thesis raises a paradox, for while there is only a single 'humanity' – that all of us, man and woman alike, partake of (and which is, after all, precisely what is attested to by the existence of truths, which as we have said are *generic*) – there are nevertheless two distinct positions of experience: the one 'masculine'; the other 'feminine'. (Badiou's approach here, it should be pointed out, is 'strictly nominalist',[5] meaning these positions are irreducible to biology.)

These two positions are moreover *absolutely* disjunct or unrelated, which is to say that '*nothing* in the experience is the same from the position of man or from that of woman'.[6] This experiential separation is, incidentally, a deeply familiar subject in the field of art – Badiou himself noting how 'art never ceases intersecting love'[7] – that is perhaps most perfectly encapsulated in the phallic objects of Alberto Giacometti's *Suspended Ball* (1930–1; Figure 8). Here, the tantalizing interplay of the two objects indicates not only the frustration of permanently deferred desire, but moreover points to the absolute disjunction of masculine and feminine positions; the fact that, while they each give the appearance of touching, they do not in fact intersect.

It follows then that the disjunction between the masculine and feminine positions is itself radically un-known, for the simple reason that all knowledge, being necessarily situated (i.e. part of the situation), must accordingly be positioned within (or *subjected to*) the disjunction itself.

In order then to be able to say anything of this disjunction, we first require a supplement in the form of an *event*. This event

Figure 8. Alberto Giacometti, *Suspended Ball* (1930-1).

is none other than the amorous *encounter*, whose trace – which generally takes the form of a declaration of love – invokes the void (or the un-known) of the disjunction (the generic statement '*I* love *you*' bringing together two fundamentally incongruous positions). Its ensuing truth is accordingly the 'treatment' of the paradox of sexual disjunction.

This invocation of the void – which, as we know, is the sole guarantee of a truth's universality – is, however, only ensured inasmuch as the trace remains an 'absolutely undetermined, non-describable, non-composable'[8] term. As such, aside from being shared across two otherwise disjunct positions, the only relation this term (*qua* eventual trace) can have is with (the) *nothing*. To this effect, love can be defined as that which *makes truth of sexual disjunction*. Or again, love makes manifest the truth that the world harbours two radically disjunct positions: love brings about the Two; it is 'the experience and thought of what the Two is'.[9]

Yet this Two must be carefully distinguished. For one thing, contra Aristophanes, it is not the Two of fusion (whereby the Two counts as One). Nor for that matter is it the Two of summation (wherein One plus One equals Two). To the contrary, the law of absolute disjunction means that neither position can have any real experience of the other, hence the impossibility of either their subsumption or addition (both of which would necessarily involve an illegal 'interiorization'). As Joan Copjec observes, 'the madness of love consists in [the] creation of Two where there never was a one and which is not itself one'.[10] Which means that, prior to love, there is no real experience of sexual difference. Or again, sex is something that only comes after the event.

From one to two

We might clarify all of this by turning to another artistic example. Like Beckett's *Film*, Alain Resnais' *Last Year in Marienbad* (1961) is a deeply enigmatic work whose plot can nonetheless be summed up surprisingly easily. At base, the film follows a man and a woman who meet at a social gathering in a baroque spa hotel. The man, *X*, attempts to convince the woman, *A*, that they met and had an affair the previous year in Marienbad (a claim that *A* steadfastly denies). Further complicating *X*'s efforts to persuade *A* of their amorous past is the presence of another man, *M*, who we presume to be *A*'s husband (though this is never confirmed).

At the level of narrative, the film thus revolves around a central enigma, namely, whether or not *X* and *A* did in fact meet and have an affair the previous year, that is to say, whether or not they *fell in love*. While the fact that this question ultimately remains unresolved has unsurprisingly been a major point of consternation for many viewers, arguably far more confounding are the experiments the film conducts at the level of its form. Indeed, *Last Year in Marienbad* is ostensibly organized around a series of formal repetitions, where events, conversations, thoughts and actions are played out again and again, at times with only the subtlest of variations. This theme extends as much to the central characters (who paradoxically replay an affair that may never have taken place) as to the hotel itself (which is depicted as an engulfing, labyrinthine structure of mirrors and baroque intricacy). *Marienbad* accordingly presents something of a *mise-en-abîme*, its credo being without doubt repetition and reflection.

It is moreover this peculiar structure that ensures *Marienbad* is a film in which time appears to stand still, seemingly forever caught replaying a single instant that stretches on to infinity. In fact, time is literally effaced in *Marienbad* in a number of immediate ways. On a superficial level, we are never told in what time the action takes place, but rather can only infer from the characters' dress and their environs (which the narrator enigmatically informs us 'belong to the past'). Likewise, while one might suppose the film to be largely constructed of jumps forward in time and flashbacks, this is never made explicit, as various discrete and frequently contradictory times (rooms seem to shift location, dress and décor alter inexplicably, incongruous events take place simultaneously...) collide in a single and same present, seemingly defeating all hope of chronologization.

It seems to me however that all of this confusion is not the result of any intentional narrative or formal impenetrability on Resnais' or scriptwriter Alain Robbe-Grillet's part, but rather stems from the fact that *Last Year in Marienbad* is situated entirely within a temporal rupture, in a 'cut' between two heterogeneous times, namely, a *pre-* and *post-eventual time*. To spell it out, *Marienbad*'s 'timeless' nature results foremost from the fact that it presents us with an *amorous event*.

No doubt my position here warrants more technical explanation. For starters, let's note that while an event's ontological illegality means that its appearance effectively coincides with its disappearance (and as such constitutes an 'ontological figure of the instant'), this does not in any way imply that it has no temporal effect. To the contrary, an event, Badiou claims, has enormous temporal consequences, insofar as it literally *splits time in two*. Or more precisely, an event interrupts one time to introduce a new time, to which he gives the name *eternal present*. In his own words, 'the event extracts from one time the possibility of an other time. This other time, whose materiality envelops the consequences of the event, deserves the name of a new present. The event is neither past nor future. It makes us present to the present'.[11]

So an event ultimately signifies a 'pure cut' in time – a break between the decaying past and the new 'eternal present' – *which is itself 'cut out' of time*. It is this peculiarly 'timeless' position that leads Badiou to describe the event variously as 'an interval of suspense',[12] 'a separating evanescence',[13] 'an atemporal instant',[14] and so on. The event itself thus vanishes *between* two radically heterogeneous times, namely, a pre-eventual and a post-eventual time. And, as suggested above, it is precisely in this properly atemporal space – in the space of the event itself – that *Marienbad* is positioned, or that its story plays out.

To be sure, the film's elliptical nature is in no way limited to time, but is equally – perhaps even more immediately – registered in its movement, which is at once incessant and directionless. *Marienbad*'s many movements (be they in-camera or of the camera itself) are, for example, characterized foremost by their possessing neither beginning nor end, being contrarily caught up in a kind of interminable passing, a passing that exists exclusively in a *present* that is without past or future. Suffice to recall the film's celebrated opening shot, in which the camera drifts (perhaps aimlessly, perhaps pointedly) along endless corridors, in a seemingly eternal movement that is ultimately reflexive of the film itself. The endless nature of this movement is further underscored by the narrator's circular monologue, which repeatedly fades in and out of existence mid-sentence, as though caught in an infinite loop, ensuring our forever being held back from knowing where the words began and where they might end.

The interminable and fundamentally *immobile* (or 'static') character of this movement – which equally extends to a physical immobility (the hotel guests having an unnerving habit of freezing mid-action, only to reanimate moments later) – might lead one to suppose that *Marienbad* presents us with an image of purgatory, if not hell. Yet it seems to me that the film should contrarily be understood as being foremost about *life*, about real creation; a subjective birth that is finally located in the amorous encounter, which is nothing other than the in(ter)vention – or the *event* – of love.

Indeed, what is *Last Year in Marienbad* if not the eternal encounter, amorous in nature, of X and A? The endlessness of this encounter lies moreover not so much in its being infinitely repeated (denied, forestalled, postponed…) as in its being *undecided*. Did X and A actually meet last year in Marienbad? And did A agree to leave M for X? This undecidability equally holds for the film's violence: did X rape A? Did M kill A?

All of these questions (which the film steadfastly refuses to answer) are themselves but subsidiary effects of *Marienbad*'s central undecidable event: are *X* and *A* in love? Simply, inasmuch as *Marienbad* is wholly contained within an amorous event, the only escape – the only way the film might truly *end* – must be through a truly decisive act, that is, in *deciding the undecidable*: either *X* and *A* *are* in love, or they *are not*. One of the masterstrokes of Resnais' film is the fact that this decision belongs as much to us (the spectators) as it does to *X* and *A*.

This central ambiguity is beautifully mirrored in the statue of the man and woman observed by *X* and *A* in the garden (a statue which, *X* notes, could as easily be of themselves). Is the man holding the woman back, protecting her from some hidden danger (*X*'s position)? Or is the woman contrarily urging him onward, toward something 'breathtaking' (*A*'s position)?

As *X* and *A* ponder this question, *M* appears to 'clarify' the situation, authoritatively stating that the statue depicts Charles III and his wife at 'the Oath before the Diet' immediately prior to his trial for treason. Thus *M*, who here clearly embodies the state, attempts to reinscribe the un-known back into the field of knowledge. And yet his explanation ultimately fails to touch upon the undecidable content of the statue, namely, on the 'truth' of the figure's (in)actions. Moreover, his story is a fabrication: while the historical markers identified by *X* appear genuine enough, no such personage existed. Simply put, statist knowledge cannot account for the undecidable. Hence the dreamlike, illogical structure of *Marienbad*: in situating itself firmly within the amorous encounter – in the undecidability of the event itself – the film effectively *subtracts itself from knowledge*. It is, I think, precisely for this reason that it still appears to this day as something of a perplexity, a mystery with no real solution, an enduring novelty. As Resnais himself puts it, *Marienbad* is an 'open film' that presents us with a choice: this is not a film to be *known*, but rather one to be *decided*.

Thus we can see how the (amorous) eventual progression from the One to the Two is what is at work in *Last Year in Marienbad*. In point of fact, this real divide separating *X* from *A* is the very source of the film's mystery, a disjunction that is principally encapsulated in what Jean-François Lyotard would call their 'differend' concerning the supposed events of the previous year. For when we get down to it, we see that *X* – whose world, as narrator (for the most part), we effectively inhabit – has no real *relationship* with *A*, even though he himself cannot know this. His is therefore a persistent (and ultimately hopeless) persuasion, a desperate imploration that *A* 'remember' him and concede to their relationship. Thus time and time again *X* attempts to bridge their sexual divide, to prove in one way or another their apparent 'connection'.

This is moreover precisely why, when confronted with *A*'s refusal to acquiesce to his own interpretation of the statue, *X* attempts to surmount their opposition by observing how both explanations may be possible at the same time, pronouncing 'the couple had left home and had been walking for days. They've just come to the edge of a cliff. He holds her back to keep her from the edge, while she points to the sea stretching out to the horizon'. Needless to say, his attempt here is fruitless: there is no existing bridge to span the sexual divide; only an evental supplement can broach this disjunction.

It is for this same reason that it is only at the close of the film, when *X* and *A* leave the hotel together – when the event is finally 'decided' (recall how Resnais famously claimed that his film presents the viewer with a pure choice) – that the Two truly emerges, this Two being attested to in the final words of the film as *X* recognizes that *A* now exists 'alone, with me'. Indeed, this 'alone, with me' encapsulates the very essence of the immanent Two (as distinct from both the 'fusional' and the 'summary' Two), the convocation whereby the void of the sexual relation invoked in the event – which is precisely what the whole of the film bears witness to – is attested to, in the opening of an amorous truth-procedure.

Thus *Last Year in Marienbad* both captures and is in turn *captured by* the eventual birth of love, which is itself nothing other than absolute fidelity to the sudden emergence of the Two, attested to in the amorous declaration '*I* love *you*', or more pointedly, 'you exist alone, with me'.

The truth of truth

We have by this stage detailed a good many important things about truth-procedures. We know, for example, that they might only come about following the sudden eruption of an event, which makes immediately apparent something that had previously been radically un-known. We also know that there are only four generic areas in which they might take place, being the fields of art, science, politics and love. And we know that they constitute, in a nutshell, active (and oftentimes hazardous) subjective sequences by which new and infinite universal truths are painstakingly constructed.

But what exactly is the nature of the truth that these procedures construct? Or more pointedly: *why* is a truth a truth? Yes, we know that a truth is an infinite generic set, but this only tells us what a truth *is*. What it does not tell us – at least not immediately – is what exactly makes a truth a truth. Or again, while we know what a truth *is*, we do not really know *what* it is.

The first and most obvious thing to point out here is that a truth is never a truth *for itself*, but is rather always the truth *of something*. Every truth comes from, and addresses, some objective space: while it makes sense to speak of 'the truth of *x*' or 'the truth of *y*', there is nothing to be gained from invoking (singular, absolute) 'Truth' (which should not be confused with the second-order 'Truth' that philosophy constructs). For, as we have repeated *ad nauseum*, truth is always the truth of the situation (or the world) whence it arises. Indeed, the most immediate reason for a truth's being 'true' lies in the fact that it says something very *particular* – even if it is at the same time essentially *universal* – about the situation out of which it emerges.

To spell it out, a truth is a truth inasmuch as it directly identifies the previously unidentified 'core' of the world in question, being the radically unpresented or in-visible cornerstone that holds everything in place. Ontologically speaking, this voided part 'founds' the situation (which it nonetheless fails to be presented in) by virtue of the fact that it constitutes the bare minimum effect of structure.

That a truth does this is a result of its fundamental relation to its void point of origin. To explain: in *Being and Event*, the eventual site – being the unique place from which the elements that form the basis of a new truth emerge – constitutes a 'radically singular' multiple, or a multiple such that *none* of its elements are situationally presented. Or again, whilst the site itself is presented (but not represented), the same cannot be said for any of its elements (all those elements huddled 'beneath' the site). Such a multiple is said to lie 'on the edge of the void',[15] because, from the situation's perspective, it is constituted solely of unpresented multiples. Or to put it another way, beneath the site there is, for all intents and purposes, *nothing*. Being a consistent multiple composed exclusively of that which in-consists (its unpresented or 'void' multiples), a site figures as the minimal effect of structure conceivable and therefore must be conceived of as *foundational*: incapable of resulting from any internal reshuffling on the part of the situation, the site requires for its existence only the minimal effect of the count. All of which is to say that the site 'founds' the situation of which it is a term.

As with our earlier consideration of the event (which, as we saw, is itself essentially a site *in extremis*), it is crucial to understand how there is nothing whatsoever mysterious about any of this. To the contrary, such a site is simply a logical consequence of the axiom of foundation, which tells us that every multiple harbours at least one element that presents nothing that the initial multiple presents (thereby prohibiting a set's belonging to itself).[16] As foundational multiples, sites – which we know constitute the very material of the event (and as such compose the core ingredients of its ensuing truth) – are fundamental to the structure of all multiplicity: simply put, every multiple is ultimately founded, and every foundation constitutes a potential site.

That a truth is a 'truth' then results from the fact that, in emerging from the site, it invokes the foundational void of the situation. And it is precisely this simultaneously disavowed yet constitutive content that is revealed as the truth of the previous situation. The truth of the readymade, for example, is that all art composes itself from non-art; that non-art is art's basic material and that there is, as such, a certain indiscernibility between these two registers. Likewise, the truth of serialism is that music of the classical and romantic period had been held hostage to an arbitrary arrangement of acoustic phenomena known as 'tonality', which finally reached a kind of structural totalization. (To be sure, while we say 'the truth of the readymade' or 'the truth of serialism', what we really mean is 'the universal truth of the artistic situation at the beginning of the twentieth century as revealed by the readymade', or 'the universal truth of the post-Wagnerian musical world as revealed by serialism'.)

In point of fact, of all of the generic procedures, it is arguably art that best illustrates how a truth is first and foremost the 'truth' of the situation in which it occurs, even as it ruptures with this situation.

That we know what pictorial representation consists in, for example, is in large part a result of the invention of non-figurative painting. That cubism – certainly one of the greatest artistic truth-procedures/sequences of the twentieth century – breaks with the previous representational system based on imitation, necessarily indicates that this was precisely what such art had consisted in (namely, greater and lesser degrees of mimesis). This simultaneous radicality and reflectivity is moreover echoed in the works themselves, Picasso and Braque's early cubist paintings – works like *Violin and Grapes* (Picasso, 1912; Figure 9), *Man with a Guitar* (Braque, 1912–13), or *Woman in a Chemise in an Armchair* (Picasso, 1913) – treading a fine line between the imperative to 'make it new', and a continuing conversation with the past. Indeed, under Picasso and Braque, cubism never moved into complete abstraction – Picasso even going so far as to argue that

Figure 9. Pablo Picasso, *Violin and Grapes* (1912).

'there is no abstract art'[17] – but rather always retained a relation (however strained) to representation and thus to the previous situation, opting instead to rethink this representative process in terms of *reconstruction* (of space into geometrical forms that are not arranged in terms of perspective; of the depth and mobility afforded by three-dimensionality subsequently fragmented and transposed unto the two-dimensional canvas).

Logically (or phenomenologically) speaking, generic procedures then speak the 'truth' inasmuch as they isolate and amplify the very foundations of the worlds in which they take place. Ontologically speaking, however, a truth *is* a truth for the simple reason that it is *generic*: its truth (or its 'universality': they are ultimately the same thing) lies in the fact that its sole characteristic is precisely the *absence* of any characteristics, meaning that it identifies with the situation as a whole. Truths speak 'for' the world because 'their being can be considered to be identical to the simple fact of belonging to this world'.[18] As Badiou nicely glosses in the preface to *Logiques des mondes*, a generic subset (*qua* truth) is identical to the entire situation for the simple reason that:

> the elements of this subset [...] have their being, or their belonging to the situation, as their only assignable property. This is what legitimates the word 'generic': a truth attests in a world to the property of being in this world. The being of a truth is the genre of being of its being.[19]

The 'truth of truth' therefore has a distinct logical and ontological constitution, each of which lies in its convocation of the foundational void: a truth is *logically* 'true' because it gives content to the void, in the form of a subjective body that 'materializes' the structural absence at the heart of the world; and it is *ontologically* 'true' because it is generic, its universality lying in the fact that it is identical to the whole of the situation by virtue of its very indiscernibility.

Or to put it more aphoristically, that a truth is *onto-logically* 'true' ultimately lies in the fact that it exposes the universal foundations of the world for all to see.

Time enough to think

If, over the course of this chapter, there is a single important concept which has arisen that has not yet been sufficiently addressed, surely it is the question of *time*. For while we have spoken of the event itself as an 'atemporal instant', discussed 'pre-' and 'post-evental' times, and even alluded to an 'eternal present', we have nonetheless not really considered 'time' itself as a philosophical concept in any real detail (and this in spite of the fact that Badiou claims that 'the distinctive service that philosophy renders thought is the evaluation of time'!)[20]

So what then is time, philosophically speaking?

First off, we cannot help but notice that there is a significant temporal dissonance at work in Badiou's fundamental philosophical concepts.

An event, for example, considered 'externally' (i.e. from a position which is not internal to the event itself) designates a *past* that is oriented toward the *future*: on the one hand, it vanishes almost as soon as it arises; while, on the other, it creates a new possibility that might only be realized in the distant future.

Conversely, a truth represents a *future* that is oriented toward the *past*: as an infinite set, a truth is necessarily 'to come'; yet as we have just seen, truth is always the truth of the previous (pre-eventual) situation, inasmuch as the event (on which a truth is founded) opens up 'the possibility of understanding the very situation in which it is produced'.[21]

A subject, for its part, is entirely caught *between* the past and the future: unfolding exclusively between the vanished event and the infinite 'to-come' of a truth, the subject exists (as we have said) in an 'eternal present'.

But how do these disparate times (past, present and future) come about? And what, moreover, do they actually mean?

We have already seen how an event splits time in two (or more precisely: how it 'extracts from one time the possibility of another'). An event is in this sense, considered 'internally' (as opposed to our previous 'external' consideration), neither past nor future, but rather something that 'presents us with the present'.[22] Further, as that which both 'decides' in the wake of a vanished event and 'indiscerns' the to-come of a truth (forcing it, as it were, *to be*), the subject is, as we know, forever caught between the *past* of the vanished event and the *future* of an unfinishable truth. The time of the subject is therefore wholly disconnected from both the past and future, being rather that of an *eternal present*. As Peter Hallward glosses, 'the time of truth is the time of a properly eternal present, indifferent to both the inheritance of the past and the promise of the future. The subject of fidelity lives exclusively in an unfolding present, the present of eventual consequences'.[23]

The time of truth (or the time of thought *per se*) is then both *eternal* – truth being precisely 'what within time exceeds time'[24] – and *immortal*, figuring the conjunction of the realm of finite and particular beings with the infinite realm of the universal. This union is arguably the most fundamental in the history of art: as Picasso avers, 'if a work of art cannot live always in the present it must not be considered at all'.[25]

It is moreover in this precise sense – namely, in our subjectivation in a truth – that Badiou can attest that '"we", of the human species, are committed to a trans-specific procedure, a procedure which opens us to the possibility of being Immortals'.[26] Or as he explains in his *Ethics*:

the fact that in the end we all die, that only dust remains, in no way alters Man's identity as immortal at the instant at which he affirms himself as someone who runs counter to the temptation of wanting-to-be-an-animal to which circumstances may expose him. And we know that every human being is *capable* of being this immortal – unpredictably, be it in circumstances great or small, for truths important or secondary. In each case, subjectivation is immortal, and makes Man.[27]

In wholly subordinating itself to the prescriptive trace of a past event, the subject 'grounds' itself in a new body oriented toward a future truth and works to produce a new eternal present, a present that signifies, properly speaking, the time of *thought*.

It is for this reason that Badiou holds philosophy to be a fundamentally *temporal* discourse. For in (re)thinking the event as something that ruptures with one time to introduce another – and in formalizing the subject-of-truth as exclusively evolving within this new time (which is entirely 'present to the present') – philosophy constructs itself around the idea of establishing a truly *contemporaneous* existence; around the possibility of producing a new present that would finally grant the subject time enough to think.

Chapter 6
Keeping the faith

We have by this stage outlined all of the crucial ingredients that go into making Badiou's philosophy, from the basic building blocks of being and appearing, up to the transgressive events, subjects and truths that break with – and are at the same time made out of – these fundamental components. So it would seem that we now have at our disposal a complete picture of Badiou's fundamentally *affirmative* philosophical system.

Being, we now know, is nothing other than multiple multiplicity. Or again, once we have denuded an object of both its context (its position in the world) and its content (all of its particular properties, qualities and attributes, together with the complex network of determinations that make it cohere as a unified object), what we arrive at is nothing other than a multiple of multiples. That such multiple multiplicity comes to appear as an object is in fact a result of its being indexed to the transcendental of a world. It is moreover not philosophy but rather science that provides the true thought of these distinct levels: mathematics in the case of being (hence a set-theoretic ontology); logic in the case of appearing (hence a category-theoretic phenomenology). Yet these orders are necessarily structurally incomplete, and their aporias designate a point at which an extra-mathematical anomaly in the form of an (aleatory, illegal) event might supplement and thereby disrupt the onto-logical calm. Creating such a disturbance, however, is not without consequence, and an event's fate is accordingly to vanish almost as soon as it appears, being drawn under by the logic of the world whose laws it contravenes. Yet even as the event is extinguished it can happen that a new subject arises from its ashes, a subject that is absolutely 'faithful' to the new possibilities that the event implies (in spite of the fact that the limited resources available in the situation mean that it cannot even be shown to have taken place), and that sets about laboriously drawing forth the manifold consequences of its having-happened, and by so doing constructs a new and universal truth.

Such is, in very broad brushstrokes, the affirmative form of Badiou's philosophy. But what can we say of its *negative* side? How do we know, for example, that an event *really was* an event? Is it not possible for a subject to constitute itself around a *false event*? And even if the event truly was an event, is there not a chance that its subject could lose sight of the bigger picture, or that it might 'lose faith' in its eternally-deferred promise? What happens then?

The (other) elephant in the room

The infamous 'street artist' Banksy has forged an enormously successful career out of subverting the artistic establishment (or the 'state of art') and focusing attention on various unpresented, inapparent parts of the world. From smuggling his own 'vandalized paintings' and other works into high profile galleries and museums, to painting ironic escapist images on the West Bank Wall (Figure 10), to lambasting the Fox network on one of its most successful programmes (*The Simpsons*), Banksy's work never fails to call attention to radically asymmetrical power relations (of elitist art institutions to its 'public'; of the state of Israel to the Palestinian territories; of multinational media corporations to, well, everyone else...).

If we were to isolate an underlying logic to Banksy's work, it would assuredly be that of the 'elephant in the room', or the

Figure 10. Banksy, *Untitled* (2005).

obvious truth hiding in plain sight that everyone studiously manages to avoid noticing or addressing. For Banksy, this logic takes many forms, from the general apathy and self-interest that allows for the continued existence of radically unequal power relations, to the absurdity of the (statist) authentication and monetization of 'street art' (which is *by definition* impermanent, unauthorized, public and free). His 2006 exhibition *Barely Legal* even went so far as to feature a live elephant, painted red and adorned with gold fleurs-de-lis (to match the wallpaper), together with a handout calling attention (if in a self-deprecating way) to world poverty and global inequality, stating:

1.7 billion people have no access to clean drinking water. 20 billion people live below the poverty line. Every day hundreds of people are made to feel physically sick by morons at art shows telling them how bad the world is but never actually doing something about it. Anybody want a free glass of wine?[1]

Given Banksy's explicit concerns with power and representation (or the lack thereof), one might reasonably expect his art to be a prime candidate for event-ness. For one thing, his works certainly shine a spotlight on what Badiou designates 'the edge of the void', namely, those parts of the world which harbour elements that are neither presented nor represented (and from which an event might emerge). More than this, in reserving his greatest ire for those cases involving organizations that attempt to conceal or publicly deny their power, it would seem that Banksy's work does everything it can to invoke and expose the all-important 'impasse of ontology' (i.e. the immeasurable amount by which a situation is 'overpowered' by its state) that underlies Badiou's conception of events and their subsequent subjects and truths. Indeed, the combined immediacy, illegality and transience of graffiti art (many of Banksy's artworks being vandalized or simply painted over soon after they appear) clearly meshes with the basic structure of the event – which, as we know, materializes out of nowhere and disappears just as quickly – while the public, 'street level' nature of this artform means that it is visibly addressed to the generic 'public figure', as opposed to the 'state representative'.

Similar parallels can also be drawn with the truth-process itself. Banksy's own carefully maintained anonymity, for example, would seem to reflect the incomprehension of the state not only with regard to the 'anonymous flash' of the event but also to its ensuing truth (recall that a truth's genericity means that it 'avoids' all criteria of discernment and thus remains 'unclassifiable for knowledge'). Likewise, his practice of repurposing (or 'reframing') common words and images – from symbolic authority figures (policemen, soldiers...) to animals (monkeys, rodents...) to works of art and popular culture (*La Gioconda*, *Pulp Fiction*...) – would appear to correspond to the subject's 'fundamental law', namely, the work of forcing (by which terms that are already present in the situation are resignified in relation to a future truth) and the consequent construction of a new subject-language.

And yet we still cannot help but wonder: is Banksy's work really as subversive as all that? To put it in more Badiouian terms: is Banksy's art truly evental, or representative of the truth-process as such? Or does it contrarily symbolize a kind of state-sanctioned insurrection? Just how 'illegal' is Banksy's art? The fact that these works are regularly auctioned off for extraordinary amounts of money, while their destruction appears to be committed more often than not by non-state representatives (be they 'rival' graffiti artists or simply mindless vandals), suggests that they enjoy an at least minimally 'legal' status. That he was given licence to rattle the Fox Broadcasting Company cage by the network itself only reinforces this point. In fact, for all his anti-statist swagger, it is hard not to conclude that Banksy has, to a large extent, been adopted – even *adapted* – by the state, and if anything, provides an excellent example of how the state 'swallows up' or *includes* (ontologically speaking) its own counter-movements with relative ease (remember that the state is, in essence, *non-political*, being rather only concerned with maintaining the status quo).

More than this, we need to keep in mind that Banksy is operating in the field of *art* (regardless of what his detractors say), while the seemingly 'evental' dimension to his work is first and foremost *political*. Although it is safe to say that his work does not add anything radically 'new' to the artistic field, drawing heavily from the earlier work of French graffiti artist Blek le Rat in particular (whose own work in fact investigates possibilities first opened up by the 'readymade-event' discussed in Chapter 3), it does however engage with the void of various political situations. Now, while the fields of art and politics can certainly become entwined – as for example in Greek tragic theatre – this in no way means that one generic condition might constitute a truth in another. Obviously art can have much to say about politics (and *vice versa*), but it is nonetheless absolutely crucial for Badiou that an artistic event can never establish a political truth.

So where exactly is the event in Banksy's work? The answer is evidently *nowhere*. This is, however, not an indictment. To the contrary, Banksy's art performs a vital service: at its best, it brings us into the presence of the void by registering its minimal existence. And yet, while indicating what is voided in the situation (the 'elephant in the room'), Banksy's works consistently fail to delve into its hidden matter. His recent semi-serious explanation behind his painting a giant kitten amidst the rubble of Gaza – because he wanted to post pictures on his website calling attention to the destruction taking place there, 'but on the Internet people only look at pictures of kittens'[2] – is a case in point: while marking a contemporary site of (political) inexistence, Banksy's kitten is nonetheless opaque (even Koons-esque), pointing as much toward the general public's inability to acknowledge the Palestinian situation as its inability to comprehend it through a work of art.

In a nutshell, Banksy's art points us toward the edge of the void without ever disclosing its contents, instead quietly – and often comically – suggesting that we go about this ourselves. That he can 'get away' with this (legally speaking) results from the fact that, even though such sites are constituted solely of unpresented multiples, the site itself is nonetheless *presented* in the situation. That is to say, it *appears* in the world in question, and thus constitutes a *minimally acceptable transgression*; an anomaly that can still be absorbed by the state.

Yet Banksy's work very much *looks* evental, bearing all the hallmarks (thus the overall *appearance*) of a truth. Which leads us to the other elephant in the room, namely, *how do we know that an event really is an event?* Is it not possible that the event to which I have dedicated myself was in fact *not* an event? Moreover, how do I know that a truth really is a truth? Insofar as an event's ensuing truth is, quite literally, the *raison d'être* of the subject, these questions must be understood as being, properly speaking, *ethical* in nature, involving issues relating not only to the constitution and continuation of the subject, but also the ultimate responsibility of the artist in the construction of their work.

While these are obviously difficult questions, as luck would have it, Badiou's brief but incendiary 1993 book *L'Ethique: Essai sur la conscience du mal* (*Ethics: An Essay on the Understanding of Evil*) goes a long way toward answering them.

The void of ethics

In a career distinguished in large part by polemy and invective, Badiou's short book on *Ethics* arguably remains to this day his most immediately provocative work (and this from a man who in 2007 published an excoriating book-length attack on the newly elected French President!). Indeed, it is difficult even for Badiou's most ardent supporters not to be at least momentarily taken aback by a book, supposedly written for a high school audience, that begins by launching into a virulent attack against the contemporary discourse of human rights, and whose axial assertion is that 'the whole ethical predication based upon recognition of the other should be purely and simply abandoned'.[3] Yet this is precisely what *Ethics* does. Exactly how it does this, however, is worth taking a moment to examine.

Badiou begins his book by identifying our contemporary ethical doxa as an ideological construction predominantly identified in terms of 'human rights'. Such an ethical conception (which finds its classical reference in the juridical philosophy of Immanuel Kant) effectively posits a universally identifiable human subject whose defining characteristic is the capacity to *suffer* (echoing, in many ways, the 'torturous' subject of Beckett's *Film*), while at the same time defining the Good as what intervenes against an *a priori* identifiable Evil (being precisely what causes the human subject to suffer: violence, enslavement, oppression, etc.). As Badiou sees it, 'human rights' are ultimately 'rights to non-Evil: rights not to be offended or mistreated with respect to one's life (the horrors of murder and execution), one's body (the horrors of torture, cruelty and famine), or one's cultural identity (the horrors of the humiliation of women, of minorities, etc.)'.[4]

Regardless of how seductive this conception of ethics may be, Badiou argues that it must be rejected as simultaneously inconsistent and standing in the way of any and all authentic human progress. Far from marking a benevolent concern with the plight of humankind, Badiou claims such an ethics contrarily serves to mask the unfettered pursuit of self-interest. Whether it does this intentionally or unintentionally is beside the point; in either case the end result is clear, being a world that is characterized by 'the disappearance or extreme fragility of emancipatory politics, the multiplication of "ethnic" conflicts, and the universality of unbridled competition'.[5]

Badiou's key objection boils down to the fact that the ethics of 'human rights' identifies man solely as a *victim*, leading to three immediate (and for Badiou, fundamentally *philosophical*) problems. First, rather than presenting an affirmative vision of humanity, this ethics reduces man to his animal, biological level (thereby relieving him of his capacity for immortality through subjectivation-in-truth). Second, in being founded on the recognition of Evil, it vilifies any and every transformative (as opposed to 'defensive') action regarding the Good as being the very source of Evil (thus prohibiting radical novelty and perpetuating a stolid conservatism). And third, in its *a priori* determination of Evil, it necessarily fails to think the situation as it truly is, relying instead on abstract and statistical frameworks (leading to an outright elimination of *thought* itself).

Today's dominant 'ethical ideology' accordingly rejects the subject (as Badiou defines it) on three separate levels: at the level of its formal possibility; at the level of the truth at which it aims; and at the level of the work that it undertakes. In short, the ideological (and fundamentally *normative*) ethics of 'human rights' stands very much in the way of the entire truth-process. Which is to say that it is, in the final analysis, an essentially 'statist ethics', being one and the same as *the ethics of the state*.

This rejection of the subject is even more evident in today's 'other' dominant understanding of ethics, namely, as the 'ethics of the other' (or of 'difference': it is the same thing). The roots of this conception lie in the work of Emmanuel Levinas – whose ethical consideration relies, it must be said, on the principal of the 'Altogether-Other', or God – while its most famous contemporary philosophical exponent is arguably Jacques Derrida.[6] Yet such venerated 'otherness' or 'difference' proves to be a fickle attribute. Indeed, the most vociferous adherents of the 'right to difference' are themselves, as Badiou points out, the first to be appalled by the spectacle of any *real* difference (one need look no further than the current wave of Islamophobia to register this fact). In actual fact, for these paragons of virtue, the 'other' is acceptable only insofar as they present a '*good* other', that is to say, if he or she is *exactly the same as them*. Or as Badiou mockingly puts it:

I respect differences, but only, of course, in so far as that which differs also respects, just as I do, the said differences. Just as there can be 'no freedom for the enemies of freedom', so there can be no respect for those whose difference consists precisely in not respecting differences.[7]

Thus the 'respect for differences' effectively designates *identity* (albeit a 'full' identity, an identity premised on recognizable properties, and not derived from the emptiness of the void) as the precondition for 'difference' to be respected. Such is the rationale, for example, underlying the standard (state-sanctioned) discourse of anti-immigration, according to which people – or to name the real subject of this discourse: *refugees* – are only welcome in a country to the extent that they fully integrate themselves into its particular ways of being and acting (that are themselves largely statist constructions), which is equally to say if they *supress their inherent differences*.

More than this, Badiou points out that 'difference', contrary to what we might think, is in fact not all that special. In actual fact, difference – which is merely another name for multiplicity as such – is simply what *is*. Any experience whatsoever is in effect an experience of difference (including, no less, my experience of myself: as Rimbaud famously averred, 'I am another'). As such, the countless 'cultural differences' over which contemporary ethics obsesses amount to little more than 'the infinite and self-evident multiplicity of humankind, as obvious in the difference between me and my cousin from Lyon as it is between the Shi'ite "community" of Iraq and the fat cowboys of Texas'.[8]

Thus Badiou determines our contemporary ethical doxa as being effectively void of ethics: while the 'ethics of human rights' is revealed to be an ideology incapable of any positive conception of the Good (yet flush with the knowledge of suffering) – the functioning of which amounts to little more than 'an intellectual justification of the status quo'[9] – the 'ethics of otherness' is likewise exposed as an indirect ethics of *identity*, whose conception of 'difference' should be understood as dubious at best.

Ethics of the void

Placing himself firmly at odds with these popular philosophies of 'otherness', Badiou demands that any conception of ethics based upon the 'recognition of the other' must be rejected outright. Indeed, when viewed through the lens of Badiou's philosophical system (and in particular his formulation of subjectivity and truth), the whole of contemporary ethics is revealed as little more than a vast synonym for negativity, today's dominant ethical ideologies of 'human rights' and 'respect for the other' being nothing other than a fundamentally statist edifice whose principal role is that of 'prohibiting any idea, any coherent project of thought, settling instead for overlaying unthought and anonymous situations with mere humanitarian prattle'.[10]

Far from buying into the fashionable 'ethics of otherness' peddled by the likes of Levinas and Derrida, Badiou defiantly champions a truly *subjective* ethics, an *ethics of the subject*, an ethics that is entirely dependent on events and the truths they (can) give rise to. For Badiou, any true ethics must converge on the process of real change, or of thought *per se* (as we have defined it). As such, true ethics – which is, it must be said, equally an ethics of truths – must be first and foremost an ethics of the *subject* and, accordingly (it amounts to the same thing), not of the Other but of the Same (which, in emanating from the situational void, is precisely what truth *is*). Meaning that Badiou's subjective ethics is, in essence, an ethics of *in-difference* (for, as we know, what a truth gives rise to is precisely that which is in-different to any and every situation). Or in other words, the only way to avoid 'the void of ethics' it to contrarily posit an *ethics of the void*.

It is hardly surprising then that Badiou strictly opposes any and every *a priori* (or normative) ethics, arguing that 'there is no ethics in general', but rather, only 'ethics of processes by which we treat the possibilities of a situation'.[11] Further, as the subject (*qua* body-of-truth) only comes into being by virtue of a singular event (which, as we know, is strictly immanent to a particular situation), and subsists only by maintaining a militant fidelity (in the face of overwhelming opposition) to the fact of the event's having-happened, then we can see that Badiou's is also ultimately a *situated ethics*, or an *ethics of the situation*.

So in sum – and in stark contrast to the dominant contemporary understanding of ethics as *natural, objective, a priori, normative* and, fundamentally, founded on *difference* and *the Other* – ethics are for Badiou *eventual, subjective, a posteriori, situational*, and, crucially, established in *in-difference* and *the Same*.

Considering the times we live in, it would seem difficult (if not outright impossible) to formulate a more polemical conception of what ethics are. And yet, like so much of his thought, this ethical disposition is nothing other than the logical consequence of Badiou's already existing philosophical theses (on truth in excess of knowledge, on the subject without object, on the same over the other, etc.).

To explain: clearly the core of Badiou's ethics is the eventual prescription of the subject, or the absolute necessity to remain faithful to a fidelity, which he rather nicely summarizes in a single imperative (derived, yet again, from Lacan): *keep going!* Plainly put, outside of the chance supplement of an event, there is *no* subject, *nor* truth *nor* ethics. Rather, there is solely difference (which, for all its 'ethical' celebration, is simply what *is*) and an otherwise inconsequential biological species counted as human; 'a "biped without feathers", whose charms are not obvious'.[12]

In light of his theory of subjectivation, Badiou accordingly reinterprets Lacan's famous ethical imperative to not 'give way on your desire'[13] as the necessity to 'seize in your being that which has seized and broken you',[14] that is, to remain faithful to the vanished event *no matter what*; to hold on at all costs to an indiscernible truth, and to never extinguish the light of the new present.

The reader of Lacan might at this point wonder precisely what is to be found here that is new? Certainly the (literally) exceptional status of Badiou's ethics resonates with Lacan's own distinction, formulated in his 1959–60 seminar on *The Ethics of Psychoanalysis*, between the 'moral' and the 'ethical': between Creon's law and Antigone's desire, or (philosophically speaking) between the Good and the Beautiful. Indeed, morality, for Lacan, fundamentally serves to reinforce the statist order (*qua* 'service of goods'), while ethics is by contrast necessarily *anti-statist*, owing to the fact that, as an ethical subject, we must first give ourself over to the cause that 'animates' us, a cause (desire, drive...) which is in itself radically antithetical to order as such. It would seem that we are once again presented with those familiar divisions between ethical radicality and moral stasis; between revolutionary praxis and conservative polity; between truth and the knowledge through which it punches a hole.

And yet it is also at this precise point that we can discern a clear break with Lacan, who we should keep in mind is, for Badiou, not only the 'antiphilosopher' *par excellence* (witness the role played here by 'desire' and the 'drives'), but also the term's true father (*'le nom du père'*, as Lacan would say). For Badiou, by virtue of his decidedly post-Lacanian (or post-Cartesian) conception of the subject, necessarily presents something of a recession of orders, seeing the ethical as being coextensive with – and indeed, equivalent to – the Good, thereby leaving morality (which is in Badiou's thinking hopelessly tied up with the truthless and fundamentally 'static' realm of opinions) lying necessarily *beneath* both Good and Evil.

Thus, in classical philosophical terms, the Beautiful descends to the Good and the Good – to invoke Badiou's reading of that other archetypal antiphilosopher, Saint Paul – falls from grace.

The faces of evil

If all of this seems somewhat negative, we should remember that one of the great virtues of Badiou's philosophy is, on the contrary, its essential *positivity*, even *optimism*, which is something we can (unexpectedly, perhaps) clearly discern in his conception of evil as being an 'effect of the power of truth'.[15] For the very idea of evil – a term which, it should be pointed out, Badiou has since conceded as being an unnecessary concession to 'the pervasive moralism of the 1980s and 1990s',[16] and has accordingly disappeared from his later work (though this in no way means that he has renounced his ethic of truths) – is, for Badiou, ultimately a potential negative consequence of the disruptive emergence of a truth.

This simple progression – *from* Good *to* Evil – stands in marked opposition to the dominant contemporary ethical ideology (espoused, for example, by the pervasive discourse of 'human rights') in which Good is solely derived on the basis of some pre-existing Evil (or where Good deprives itself of positive content in its reduction to the solitary function of *preventing* Evil), which accordingly thinks 'the only thing that can really happen to someone is death'.[17] As Badiou himself puts it, 'I've had enough of "fighting against," of "deconstructing," of "surpassing," of "putting an end to," etc. My philosophy desires affirmation. I want to fight for; I want to know what I have for the good and to put it to work'.[18] Simply, if the ultimate aim of the Good is nothing other than truth, then Evil must be, at base, that which has a negative effect on truth: it is the *corruption* in one way or another of truth.

Thus we can say that the human animal, along with its concomitant predilections – be they munificent, disinterested, or just plain mean – exists, outside of its subjective incorporation, fundamentally *beneath* Good and Evil.

But the Good should not be confused with truth itself. Rather, what Badiou designates the Good is in fact the absolute fidelity of a subject to an event, the roots of which lie in the amorous condition, Badiou noting that 'the subjective process of a truth is one and the same thing as the love for that truth'.[19] Or to take it one step further, what the Good designates, in Platonic terms, is the *event itself* – 'the point of radical alterity at which all referrals and all relations come to be suspended' and which 'is consequently subtracted from both the Idea and exposition'[20] – meaning the ethical imperative is not so much that of 'being good' as that of *remaining faithful to the Good*.

And yet, as we have suggested, from Good comes Evil (even if this specific term is no longer retained by Badiou), and such evil comes in three forms, namely: *betrayal, terror* and *disaster*.

The first, *betrayal*, simply denotes a crisis of fidelity, or the failure of a subject to live up to the extraordinary demands of an event: works produced in an artistic sequence become increasingly sterile and derivative; after countless arguments the lovers begin to question their commitment to one another; years of painstaking research lead to no substantial breakthrough and a scientific theory loses its clarity; revolutionary ideals gradually disappear as the militant is worn down by the bitter realities of the 'political system'. Confronted with such a 'point' (in the philosophical sense), the subject can either hold fast to the ethical imperative and 'keep going' (that is, remain a faithful subject), or they can turn tail and run. Yet to turn one's back on a truth – to 'rupture with the rupture' – is not simply to renounce it; to the contrary, it is to become the 'enemy of that truth'.[21] For to 'break' with a truth is equally to affirm the *continuity* of the situation, which is precisely what its truth deposes. Thus the betrayal of a truth is at the same time the determined act of becoming its enemy.

The second form of evil, which Badiou calls *'terror'*, presents itself on the other hand as the gross imitation of the event, the fidelity to which leads only to the 'simulacrum' of a truth. In explaining this evil, Badiou gives the example of the Nazi 'National Socialist Revolution' which, while nominally drawing upon an authentic political history ('socialism', 'revolution'…), in doing so altogether fails to draw forth the void of the situation and instead grounds itself in its particularity, in the 'German people' and their destiny, which is rooted in ideas of soil, blood and race. In short, 'terror' lies in a kind of 'false event' – a *non-event* that bears the superficial appearance of an event – which involves the convocation not of the void (whose in-difference alone allows for the universality of a truth) but rather of the plenitude of a situation.

Lastly, the evil of *disaster* (or of 'totalization') results from going too far: put simply, a subject cannot force *everything* in the situation; there will always remain inconsequential elements, terms that cannot be treated as an evental consequence, objects that have no relation whatsoever to the evental trace. To force such elements to dispose themselves as being in some way connected to the event is to risk the evil of 'disaster'. In this last sense the corruption of a subject lies in 'the process of treating as a possible consequence of an event something that is not in fact a consequence'.[22]

In sum, Evil exists, *après l'événement*, in three guises: betrayal, or the negation of the ethical imperative (in the form of evental treachery); terror, or the convocation of the plenitude of the situation (as distinct from its void); and disaster, or the totalization of a truth (by forcing inconsequential objects to be consequential).

That said, as we telegraphed earlier, Badiou has at least partially reformulated his ethics of truths so as to reclassify evil as a properly *subjective* modality. Or again, he has now reconsidered the problem of 'Evil' in terms of the 'subjective' corruption of a truth. Accordingly, Badiou has in his recent work come to distinguish four different possible subjective modalities (only two of which are 'Good'), which he designates, in order of their emergence, *faithful, reactionary, obscure* and *resurrected*.

Beginning on a positive note, the *faithful subject* is the subject we are already intimately familiar with, namely, the subject who, in wholly subordinating itself to the prescriptive trace of the event, 'grounds' itself in a new body and works to produce, under the name of 'truth', a new eternal present (recall that the subject 'lives exclusively in an unfolding present', being forever caught between the past of a vanished event and the future of an unfinishable truth).

The *reactive subject* (which reworks the problem of 'betrayal') contrarily seeks to extinguish this present through the active negation – as opposed to the simple disavowal – of the trace of the event. The reactive subject thus counters the 'evental present' of the faithful subject by constructing an alternative present. Far removed from 'the glorious and affirmative present of the faithful subject', this 'reactive' present is rather 'a measured present, a negative present, a present "a little less worse" than the past'.[23]

The *obscure subject* – which rethinks the evil of 'terror' – however goes one step further by seeking the outright annihilation of the evental present, invoking in its place a transcendent 'incorruptible and indivisible over-body, be it City, God or Race'.[24] That the obscure subject calls forth such a 'full body' attests to its invocation not of the void but rather the full particularity of a situation, in the hope that the 'true' eventual trace will be denied. Indeed, Badiou claims it is the fervent desire of the obscure subject to obliterate the new present in deference to an obscure past.

In sum, the faithful, reactive and obscure subjects each constitute themselves with regard to a new present: first we have the faithful subject which *produces* the new present; next, there is the reactive subject which organizes its *denial*; and then there is the obscure subject which arranges its *occultation*.

All of which leads us finally to the fourth possible modality of the subject, namely, the *resurrected subject*. For even after it has been denied and occulted, it is still possible to breathe new life into the present, even if this must take place in another world and through another event (which leads to a new trace and a new body…). Badiou thus calls 'resurrection' the *reactivation* of a subject in another logic of its appearing-in-truth. In a word, while the reactive subject denies the trace and thereby extinguishes the present, and the obscure subject organizes its occultation (thus eliding the present), the resurrected subject testifies to the present's inexpugnability, to its ineradicable *eternity*, which is, after all, 'nothing other than the presence of the present'.[25]

Beneath good and evil

In the face of Badiou's reformulation of evil in terms of possible subjective modalities (whereby 'betrayal' and 'disaster' are respectively reconsidered as reactive and obscure subjective orientations) one cannot fail to note that the evil of 'terror' does not rate a mention. This is because these 'evil' subjects designate the ways in which a truth is corrupted, whereas the defining feature of 'terror' is not truth but rather its *simulacrum*. As such, terror can in no way constitute a subjective position; there is no 'subject of terror' for the simple reason that terror indicates the very absence of subjectivity.

And yet, of the key 'resources' Badiou claims his ethics presents us with – namely, those of 'discernment (do not fall for simulacra), of courage (do not give up), and of moderation (do not get carried away to the extremes of totality)'[26] – it is arguably the first, *discernibility* (in the face of 'terror'), that presents the most immediate problem. To put it bluntly: as the event is radically unknowable there remains the dilemma of precisely how we are able to discern when it is that we are truly 'immortalized' in its wake. Or again, how can we be certain that we are subject to Good (truth) and not Evil (the simulacrum of truth), or, conversely, to neither (and hence 'unsubjected')?

Of course the discernment Badiou is speaking of here relates to the key difference between terror and true (subjective) fidelity in terms of what they separately convoke: while terror grounds itself in the plenitude of the situation, a true event contrarily brings forth its void. Yet discerning the difference between these two is obviously easier said than done! For, while prior to the event the void remains absolutely inapparent and thus fundamentally *unknown*, the very action of the event is to reverse this situation, making it maximally apparent; suddenly what was voided assumes absolute priority in the world, and thus signifies, in a sense, the very fullness of the situation. Spotting the difference between the relative 'fullness' of a true event and a non-event is then no small task.

Badiou himself obliquely hints at this problem when he proposes something of an extended ethical maxim in the form of 'keep going even when you have lost the thread, when you no longer feel 'caught up' in the process [...] or when it seems that it may have named a mistake, if not a simulacrum'.[27] And indeed, do we not encounter in the intricately linked evils of betrayal and terror (or of the reactive subject and, for lack of a better word, the *false* subject) a kind of ethical bind, insofar as, in our militant desire to be ethical subjects, might we not all too easily remain faithful to a simulacrum for fear of betrayal (or, contrariwise, betray a truth for fear of its being a simulacrum)?

Properly speaking, this question is less one of discernibility than of *indiscernibility*. For given the fact that truth (like the event on which it is constructed) is, by definition, radically subtracted from knowledge, it is accordingly relegated to the realm of pure subjectivity, which is to say, *pure faith* (specifically, the subjective fidelity involved in declaring an indiscernible event 'to be or not to be'). This pure faith is ultimately one and the same as that faith which constitutes the deadlock of betrayal and terror, namely, the conviction – or lack thereof – that an event is in fact an event and not its simulacrum.

Let us put it yet another way: truth, Badiou tells us – as radically subtracted from knowledge – is utterly unforeseeable and (ontologically speaking) solely a matter of *forcing*. A truth exists only by virtue of a tireless militancy, the direct result of which is that Badiou's ethics – under those resources of 'discernment' and 'courage' – seems to have a decidedly *un*-ethical element (namely the potential indiscernibility between event and simulacra, between betrayal and terror), which is finally to say that ethics is in some sense *beneath itself*.

So where does this leave Badiou's ethics? Certainly he brings us a long way from the fallacy of our contemporary ethical doxa (where ethics appears objective, natural, normative, etc.) as an ideology incapable of any conception of the Good yet flush with the knowledge of suffering. Yet his own ethics (of the subject, of the event, of the situation, etc.) seem to rest on – to give a different accent to the final lines of Samuel Beckett's *The Unnamable* – the indiscernibly fine line which separates 'I can't go on' from 'I'll go on'.

Perhaps then it all finally comes down, as Badiou's philosophical contemporary Deleuze might have said, to a matter of taste. For when all is said and done, the properly decisive elements Badiou presents us with – both subjective (in deciding an answer to the question 'to betray or not to betray?') and constitutive (in his philosophy's overall militant immediacy) – are arguably major drawcards of his thought. Given that Badiou ultimately presents little to no room for hesitation – there is no: 'what should I do?'; there is only: '*this is what I will do*' – the fact that there is an element of ethical indiscernibility (or an 'ethical real') appears to be, at worst, a necessary Evil supplementary to a greater Good (truth, creation, affirmation, etc.), and at best, the locus of *freedom itself*.

Indeed, this indiscernible element in truth complements rather nicely the idea of evil as totalization (or of the obscure subject), an evil whose origins might be, at least theoretically, traced all the way to Badiou's fundamental axiom that *the one is not*. Put plainly, truth, insofar as it obliges subjective indiscernibility, is simply nothing without risk.

If indiscernibility, forced through an act of pure decision, marks Badiou's rigorous – and, not insignificantly, *axiomatic* – philosophical system with a certain freedom (admittedly tempered somewhat by one's subsequent slavish devotion to the evental trace and necessary indifference to self-interest), it is only because his doctrine of the event stamps his world with an element of chance.

For as we have seen, Badiou's is a Mallarméan philosophy of dice-throws, of infinities and immortality, one that thinks radical newness and absolute change. And fundamentally, his is a hazardous philosophy, a philosophy of risks. In the final analysis, it is perhaps this uncertain fact, this absolute unknown, that alone endows the immortal subject with a certain humanity.

Conclusion
Badiou reframed

At the very beginning of this book – on the *very first page*, no less – we noted that Badiou is one of the most polarizing philosophers writing today, before going on to assert that such polemicizing is in fact an essential function of philosophy as well as of thought itself.

Exactly why any and every instance of authentic thought is necessarily polemical should by now be abundantly clear. As Badiou is at pains to point out, 'every truth' – which is precisely what all real thought (artistic or otherwise) aims at – 'deposes constituted knowledges, and thus opposes opinions. For what we call *opinions* are representations without truth, the anarchic debris of circulating knowledge'.[1] Simply put, there can be no 'opinions' concerning truth: either something is 'for the truth', or it is not (and is accordingly 'truthless'). This divisiveness is moreover inherent to the very structure of a subjective truth-procedure (which, as we know, is simply another name for 'thought'), whose backbone is constituted through a series of crucial *points* at which the infinite possibilities of a world boil down into a single 'yes' or 'no' option; where the entire world is filtered through the polarizing lens of a new truth.

Likewise, as we said at the start of the last section, that philosophy's sole object is truth means that it does not constitute a form of conversation. This is ensured by the simple fact that the truths which philosophy seizes, as we have said, cut a swathe through the field of opinions. Accordingly, Badiou makes no apologies for the polemical and even combative nature of his work. Nor, for that matter, does he offer any concessions. Philosophy is not a space of agreement and compromise. To the contrary, philosophy is more akin to a 'battlefield', being the very space in which the fight to transform contemporary subjectivity takes place.

This battle plays out on many fronts, not least in the field of *innovation*. Few for example would dispute the fact that Badiou's is a truly innovative philosophy, both in the sense that it presents us with new ways of constituting and comprehending real thought, and in that it confronts the question of novelty head on. Yet this novel focus organizes an aggressive dialectic between, on the one hand, *affirmation* (the declaration of the existence of something radically new – a true artistic innovation, a political revolution…), and on the other, *negation* (the cancelling out of something that already exists). As we have seen, this tension between affirmation and negation (or between 'creation' and 'destruction') is not incidental but rather absolutely central to Badiou's thought, being one of the rigorously drawn-out consequences of his complex philosophical system.

It is, perhaps more than anything else, this last point – the fact that Badiou truly presents us with a *system*, in the deep sense of the word – that ensures the divisive nature of his work. For Badiou's is not simply a systematic philosophy. More than this, it is a *systematically polemical philosophy*. Or again, if Badiou is polarizing, he is *rigorously so*.

To take only a single example: that the discourse of 'human rights' and the accompanying 'ethics of otherness' must be rejected is, as we saw in the last chapter, a direct consequence of another equally polarizing thesis, namely, his conceptualization of a truth-procedure, which is moreover rooted in his post-Cartesian conception of the subject, that is itself the upshot of his formulation of events and truths, which in turn result from his equation of ontology with mathematics, that is likewise derived from Cantor's formalization of the infinite and consequent invention of set theory as well as Badiou's own inaugural decision regarding the one and the multiple [...] It is plain to see how each and every step along this path is itself divisive: that a truth-procedure disrupts economies of knowledge and radically affects the very foundations of the situation; that the only acceptable conception of the subject is as a formal structure; that truths exist (and that they are both constructed and generic); that events can happen (and that they are both aleatory and illegal); that ontology *is* mathematics; that the one *is not*...

This is in fact the last sense by which we might 'reframe' Badiou – outside of the visual arts; outside of the ontological recapitulation of a situation; outside of the philosophical 'seizure' of truths – namely, as a systematic thinker of absolute, non-synthesizable, division. Or, more controversially: as a *non-dialectical dialectician*. For even though Badiou designates his own philosophy a 'materialist dialectic' (hinging on the statement that 'there are only bodies and languages, *except that there are truths*'), this does not annul the fact that the truths which the generic conditions produce (and that philosophy accordingly seizes) are themselves essentially *non-dialecticizable*. Indeed, the 'dialectic' here refers first and foremost to that between *being* and *event*, while its synthetic result – in the form of a new *truth* – is itself, as Badiou asserts, *eternal*: once established, a truth is available, indivisibly and universally, for all time.

This, so far as I am concerned, is where the real strength of Badiou's philosophy finally resides: in the fact that it directly opposes the consensual (and fundamentally conservative) rule of opinion with the divisive (and non-dialecticizable) law of truth. Or, to put it in more 'artistic' terms: in the way that it sets out a coherent framework that not only allows us to recognize true artworks as simultaneously undermining and transcending the accepted art of the time, but moreover exposes this 'acceptable' art for the statist affair that it is. For what is art if not the radical creation or *formation* of a new absolute that, at one and the same time, marks the destitution (if not the outright destruction) of the existing artistic establishment?

To this end, far from being condemned, the polarizing nature of philosophy, of art, and of thought in general is to the contrary something that needs to be celebrated! For a world without real polemics, or – it is the same thing – a world without *thought*, is equally a world without conviction, without creation, and without alternative. In short, it is a world without truth.

It is the great virtue of Badiou's philosophy that it shows us that we do not have to settle for such a world. All we have to do is begin to think for ourselves.

Notes

Introduction

1 Badiou, Alain, *Being and Event*, trans. Oliver Feltham (London: Continuum, 2005): 4.
2 Badiou, Alain, and Fabien Tarby, *Philosophy and the Event*, trans. Louise Burchill (Cambridge: Polity Press, 2013): 104.
3 Badiou, Alain, and Bruno Bosteels, 'Can change be thought: a dialogue with Alain Badiou', *Alain Badiou: Philosophy and its Conditions*, ed. Gabriel Riera (New York: SUNY Press, 2005): 252–3.
4 Ibid.: 253.
5 Badiou, Alain, *Logics of Worlds: Being and Event, 2*, trans. Alberto Toscano (London: Continuum, 2009): 369.
6 Lacan, Jacques, *The Seminar of Jacques Lacan, Book I: Freud's Papers on Technique 1953–1954*, ed. Jacques-Alain Miller, trans. John Forrester (New York: Norton, 1991): 228.

Chapter 1

1 Badiou, *Being and Event*: 4.
2 Ibid.: 36.
3 Badiou, Alain, *Briefings on Existence: A Short Treatise on Transitory Ontology*, trans. Norman Madarasz (New York: SUNY, 2006): 34, trans. modified.
4 Badiou, *Being and Event*: 95.
5 Badiou, Alain, *Number and Numbers*, trans. Robin Mackay (London: Polity, 2008): 2.
6 The influential American art critic Clement Greenberg famously held that in modernism 'the unique and proper area of each art coincided with all that was unique to the nature of its medium... Thereby each art would be rendered "pure", and in its "purity" find the

guarantee of its standards of quality as well as of its independence', Clement Greenberg, 'Modernist Painting', *Art in Theory 1900–2000: An Anthology of Changing Ideas*, ed. Charles Harrison & Paul Wood (Oxford: Blackwell, 2003): 775.

7 Badiou, Alain, *The Century*, trans. Alberto Toscano (Cambridge: Polity, 2007): 53.

8 Ibid.: 55.

9 Ibid.: 132.

10 Badiou, Alain, 'Drawing', *Lacanian Ink* 28 (2006): 44.

11 ZFC stands for Zermelo-Fraenkel set theory with the Axiom of Choice, being the branch of mathematics that is by far the most frequently employed foundational system of mathematics. It is worth noting that Badiou does not hold ZFC to be the *only* possible discourse on being (and as such the only possible ontology), but rather the best system available: that ontology 'is historically accomplished as a mathematics of multiplicities' (Badiou, *Second Manifesto for Philosophy*: 29) does not demand in any way that set theory *alone* provides this structure; it is always conceivable that something better will come along.

12 Badiou, Alain, *Handbook of Inaesthetics*, trans. Alberto Toscano (Stanford, California: Stanford University Press, 2005): 22.

13 Hausdorff, Felix, *Set Theory* (New York: Chelsea Publications, 1962): 11.

14 ZFC thus provides further mathematical support for our assertion that the void figures the proper name of being. Other pertinent aspects of ZFC that we cannot explore here include its axiomatic (i.e. non-derivative, non-deductive, non-intuitive) nature; the fact that it is entirely expressed in first-order logic and that all of its concepts are defined intrinsically; that it possesses only one existential axiom (the axiom of the void); that it is non-descriptive and non-empirical; and that it axiomatically constructs its universe from the void alone (through the axiom of the power set).

15 Badiou, Alain, *Mathematics of the Transcendental*, ed. & trans. A.J. Bartlett & Alex Ling (London: Bloomsbury, 2014): 165.

16 Hallward, Peter, *Badiou: A Subject to Truth* (London: University of Minnesota Press, 2003): 293–294.

17 By 'onto-logical' Badiou effectively condenses the two major axioms of *Being and Event* and *Logics of Worlds*, namely, that 'mathematics is ontology' (Badiou, *Being and Event*: 4) and that '"logic" and "consistency of appearing" are one and the same thing' (Badiou, *Logics of Worlds*: 38). On a technical note, 'onto-logy' equally designates a *separation* (of ontology from logic; of being from appearing) as well

as an *intrication*, inasmuch as the logic that Badiou is concerned with is itself ontologically – that is to say, mathematically – prescribed (as opposed to ordinary formal or linguistic logic).

18 Badiou, Alain, *Conditions*, trans. Stephen Corcoran (London: Continuum, 2008): 60.

19 Ibid.: 60.

20 Malevich, Kasimir, 'From cubism to futurism to suprematism: the new realism in painting', *Art in Theory 1900–2000: An Anthology of Changing Ideas*, ed. Charles Harrison & Paul Wood (Oxford: Blackwell, 2003): 181.

21 Badiou, *Logics of Worlds: Being and Event, 2*: 194.

Chapter 2

1 Badiou, Alain, and Lauren Sedofsky, 'Matters of appearance: an interview with Alain Badiou', *Artforum* 45/3 (2006): 322.

2 Badiou, Alain, *Deleuze: The Clamor of Being*, trans. Louise Burchill (Minneapolis: University of Minnesota Press, 2000): 21.

3 Badiou, Alain, *Metapolitics*, trans. Jason Barker (London: Verso, 2005): xxxix.

4 Badiou, *Handbook of Inaesthetics*: xiv.

5 Badiou's work on cinema is frequently sidelined or simply written-off in secondary scholarship. To take a single but telling example, Peter Hallward – in whom Badiou recognizes his 'most well-versed and ardent interpreter and critic' (Badiou, *Logics of Worlds: Being and Event, 2*: 543) – in his seminal work *Badiou: A Subject to Truth* contends that, unlike the other arts, 'Badiou is not entirely convinced of the artistic potential of film' (Hallward, *Badiou: A Subject to Truth*: 206), and accordingly grants cinema only a single page entry in his nigh-on five-hundred page tome. Aside from a smattering of papers that critically engage with Badiou's work on cinema, the only sustained response to Badiou's work on film remains my own *Badiou and Cinema* (Alex Ling, *Badiou and Cinema*, Edinburgh: Edinburgh University Press, 2011).

6 Cf. Badiou, Alain, *Cinema*, ed. Antoine de Baecque, trans. Susan Spitzer (Cambridge: Polity Press, 2013).

7 Badiou, Alain, 'La culture cinématographique', *Vin Nouveau* 5 (1957): 3–22. Cf. Badiou, *Cinema*, 21–33.

8 Badiou, Alain, and Elie During, 'Le 21e siècle n'a pas commencé: entretien avec Elie During', *Art Press* 310 (2005): 58.

9 Badiou, *Cinema*: 233.

10 Bazin, André, *What is Cinema?: Volume 2*, ed. & trans. Hugh Gray (Berkeley, California: University of California Press, 1971): 98.

11 Bazin, André, *What is Cinema?: Volume 1*, ed. & trans. Hugh Gray (Berkeley, California: University of California Press, 1967): 13.

12 Badiou, *Cinema*: 201.

13 Ibid.: 233.

14 Ibid.: 201.

15 Badiou, *Handbook of Inaesthetics*: 79.

16 Badiou, *Logics of Worlds: Being and Event, 2*: 204.

17 Ibid.: 205.

18 Badiou, Alain, 'Towards a new concept of existence', *Lacanian Ink* 29 (2007): 68.

19 Dolar, Mladen, 'Hitchcock's objects', *Everything You Always Wanted to Know About Lacan (But Were Afraid to Ask Hitchcock)*, ed. Slavoj Žižek (London: Verso, 1992): 45.

20 Badiou, *Logics of Worlds: Being and Event, 2*: 231.

21 Badiou, Alain, 'Rhapsody for the theatre: a short philosophical treatise', *Theatre Survey*, trans. Bruno Bosteels, 49/2 (2008): 188.

22 Beckett, Samuel, *Samuel Beckett: The Complete Dramatic Works* (London: Faber and Faber, 1990): 323.

23 Badiou, Alain, *On Beckett*, ed. & trans. Alberto Toscano & Nina Power (Manchester: Clinamen, 2003): 16.

24 Ibid.: 107–8.

25 Ibid.: 11.

26 Ibid.: 11.

27 Ibid.: 52.

28 Beckett, *Samuel Beckett: The Complete Dramatic Works*: 323.

29 Badiou, *On Beckett*: 12.

30 Ibid.: 53.

31 Ibid.: 53.

32 Ibid.: 11.

33 Schneider, Alan, 'On directing film', *Film by Samuel Beckett* (London: Faber and Faber, 1972): 88.

34 Feshbach, Sidney, 'Unswamping a backwater: on Samuel Beckett's *Film*', *Samuel Beckett and the Arts: Music, Visual Arts, and Non-Print Media*, ed. Lois Oppenheim (New York: Garland Publishing, 1999): 355.

35 Deleuze, Gilles, *Essays Critical and Clinical*, trans. Daniel W. Smith & Michael A. Greco (Minneapolis: University of Minnesota Press, 1997): 26.

36 Critchley, Simon, 'To be or not to be is not the question: on Beckett's *Film*', *Film-Philosophy*, 11/2 (2007): 113.

37 Deleuze, Gilles, *Cinema 1: The Movement-Image*, trans. Hugh Tomlinson & Barbara Habberjam (London: Continuum, 2005): 70.

38 Critchley, 'To be or not to be is not the question: on Beckett's *Film*': 111.

39 Beckett, *Samuel Beckett: The Complete Dramatic Works*: 323.

40 Deleuze, *Cinema 1: The Movement-Image*: 70.

41 Deleuze, *Essays Critical and Clinical*: 25.

42 Deleuze, *Cinema 1: The Movement-Image*: 70.

43 Badiou, *Cinema*: 201.

Chapter 3

1 Badiou, *Being and Event*: 181.

2 As Badiou observes, 'the state is an entity that has only one idea: to persevere in its being', Alain Badiou and Marcel Gauchet, *What Is To Be Done?: A Dialogue on Communism, Capitalism, and the Future of Democracy*, trans. Susan Spitzer (Cambridge: Polity Press, 2016): 40. It is worth reiterating here that the ontological 'state' is irreducible to its political namesake: as we saw in Chapter 2, the 'state' simply designates the ontological 'superstructure' of the situation, being the double structuring or 'count of the count' by which the structure of a situation is itself 'counted as one', thereby ensuring that there is both (situated) presentation and (statist) *re*-presentation. That said, while the state itself (*qua* structural re-count) necessarily remains 'unintentional', the same need not apply for the various organizations – such as the parliamentary state, or (as we will see momentarily) certain artistic institutions – that might serve as its *placeholder*.

3 Badiou, *Being and Event*: 198.

4 Ibid.: 189.

5 Badiou, *Logics of Worlds: Being and Event, 2*: 369.

6 Ibid.: 363.

7 Ibid.: 452.

8 This is perhaps the most conspicuous 'switch' between *Being and Event* and *Logics of Worlds*, as in the former work it was in fact the *event* – as opposed to (and entirely distinct from) its site – which constituted the paradoxical reflexive multiple (being composed of all the unpresented elements of the site and itself). In *Logics of Worlds* however Badiou is able to fundamentally identify the event with the site. Or more precisely, Badiou demonstrates that a site *can be* an event. Obviously this identification involves a significant revision of his earlier claim

that 'an event is not (does not coincide with) an eventual site' (Badiou, *Being and Event*: 182).

9 Badiou, *Logics of Worlds: Being and Event, 2*: 369.
10 Badiou, Alain, *Ethics: An Essay on the Understanding of Evil*, trans. Peter Hallward (London: Verso, 2001): 73.
11 Badiou, *Logics of Worlds: Being and Event, 2*: 384.
12 Duchamp, Marcel, *The Writings of Marcel Duchamp*, eds. Michel Sanouillet & Elmer Peterson (New York: De Capo Press, 1989): 140.
13 See De Duve, Thierry, *Kant After Duchamp* (Cambridge, Massachusetts: MIT Press, 1996): 128.
14 Louise Norton, 'Buddah of the bathroom', *The Blind Man* 2 (1917): 5.
15 Duchamp, *The Writings of Marcel Duchamp*: 142.
16 Tomkins, Calvin, *Marcel Duchamp: The Afternoon Interviews* (Brooklyn: Badlands Unlimited, 2013): 17.
17 Duchamp in De Duve, *Kant After Duchamp*: 162.
18 Badiou, *Handbook of Inaesthetics*: xiv.
19 Ibid.: 13.
20 Badiou, Alain, and Lauren Sedofsky, 'Being by numbers', *Artforum* 33/2 (1994): 124.
21 Unattributed, 'The Richard Mutt Case', *The Blind Man* 2 (1917): 3–4.
22 While one may suppose *Fountain* to constitute a kind of 'sculpture' – its presentation in Stieglitz's famous photograph (where it sits atop a plinth) certainly suggesting as much – this is in no way incontestable. Alex Potts, for example, conceives of the readymades' power as lying predominantly in their photographic reproductions (Alex Potts, *The Sculptural Imagination: Figurative, Modernist, Minimalist* (New Haven: Yale University Press, 2000): 114–117), while Thierry de Duve convincingly argues that the readymade is rather an extension of the field of painting, Thierry De Duve, *Pictorial Nominalism: On Marcel Duchamp's Passage from Painting to the Readymade*, trans. Dana Polen (Minneapolis: University of Minnesota Press, 1991).
23 Potts, *The Sculptural Imagination: Figurative, Modernist, Minimalist*: 114.
24 Formis, Barbara, 'Event and ready-made: delayed sabotage', *Communication & Cognition*, 27/3 (2004): 254.
25 Duchamp, Marcel, *Notes*, ed. Paul Matisse (Boston: G. K. Hall, 1983): unpaginated.
26 De Duve, Thierry, *Pictorial Nominalism: On Marcel Duchamp's Passage from Painting to the Readymade*, trans. Dana Polen (Minneapolis: University of Minnesota Press, 1991): 160.

27 Badiou, *The Century*: 55.
28 Formis, 'Event and ready-made: delayed sabotage': 254.
29 Ibid.: 255.
30 Badiou, Alain, 'Some remarks concerning Marcel Duchamp', *The Symptom* 9 (2008), http://www.lacan.com/symptom9_articles/badiou29.html (accessed 14 July 2016).
31 Badiou, Alain, *Polemics*, ed. & trans. Steve Corcoran (London: Verso, 2006): 146.
32 Ibid.: 146.
33 Duchamp, *The Writings of Marcel Duchamp*: 142.

Chapter 4

1 While a multiple-set β *belongs* to another multiple-set α (i.e. $\beta \in \alpha$) if it enters into α's multiple-composition (that is, if β is an element of α), a multiple-set β is equally *included* in a multiple-set α if *all* of its elements are also elements of α (i.e. $\beta \subset \alpha$). Metaontologically (or philosophically) speaking, belonging refers to presentation while inclusion refers to (statist) representation.
2 That the void 'insists' in the situation should be understood in at least two senses: first, it forces (or 'insists upon') its own inclusion in the situation in spite of its prohibited status (the state's primary role being that of *excluding* the void); and second, being 'void', it does not 'consist' of anything – in fact, it doesn't consist *at all* – but rather 'inconsists' or 'in-sists'.
3 Badiou reasons that, 'given that no immanent limit anchored in the one determines multiplicity as such, there is no originary principle of finitude. The multiple can therefore be thought of as in-finite. Or even, infinity is another name for multiplicity as such', Badiou, *Briefings on Existence: A Short Treatise on Transitory Ontology*: 45, trans. modified.
4 Badiou, *Ethics: An Essay on the Understanding of Evil*: 25.
5 Badiou, *Being and Event*: 278.
6 Ibid.: 280.
7 Badiou, *Logics of Worlds: Being and Event, 2*: 4.
8 Ibid.: 144.
9 Badiou, *Briefings on Existence: A Short Treatise on Transitory Ontology*: 60 (trans. modified)
10 Badiou, *Being and Event*: 191.
11 Badiou, *Logics of Worlds: Being and Event, 2*: 4.
12 Mallarmé, Stéphane, *Collected Poems*, trans. Henry Weinfield (Berkeley: University of California Press, 1994): 130.

13. Ibid.: 121.
14. Badiou, *Being and Event*: 193.
15. Ibid.: 193.
16. Mallarmé, *Collected Poems*: 126.
17. Ibid.: 126.
18. Ibid.: 130–2.
19. Ibid.: 142.
20. Ibid.: 138–41.
21. Ibid.: 136–8.
22. Ibid.: 144.
23. Ibid.: 144.
24. Badiou, *Being and Event*: 197.
25. Mallarmé, *Collected Poems*: 144.
26. Badiou, *Being and Event*: 197.
27. Ibid.: 197.
28. Mallarmé, *Collected Poems*: 144.
29. To be clear, in *Being and Event* this connection is actually made between a situation's constituent multiples and the 'name of the event' which, being attributed by a subject, is accordingly less an evental trace than the subjective *tracing* of the event. In *Logics of Worlds* however Badiou abandons this 'recourse to a mysterious naming' (Badiou, *Logics of Worlds: Being and Event, 2*: 361) in favour of a 'less miraculous' evental trace.
30. Badiou, *Being and Event*: 233.
31. Badiou, *Logics of Worlds: Being and Event, 2*: 470.
32. Badiou, *Being and Event*: 11.
33. Badiou, *Logics of Worlds: Being and Event, 2*: 73.
34. Duchamp in Tomkins, *Marcel Duchamp: The Afternoon Interviews*: 30.
35. Badiou, *Being and Event*: 14.
36. Badiou, *Logics of Worlds: Being and Event, 2*: 80.
37. Ibid.: 80.
38. Ibid.: 81.
39. Ibid.: 81.
40. In extremely reductive terms, the generic set 'avoids' every nameable (thus statist) property in the situation by ensuring that, for each and every property, it contains at least one element that negates this property, as well as at least one that affirms the same property (the latter being, as we will see, ultimately its very *being*). The end result being that it constitutes 'a hole, or subtraction, in the field of the nameable', Badiou, *Manifesto for Philosophy*: 104.
41. Badiou, *Being and Event*: 338.

42 Ibid.: 339.
43 Ibid.: 339.
44 Ibid.: 410.
45 Bartlett, A. J., *Badiou and Plato: An Education by Truths* (Edinburgh: Edinburgh University Press, 2011): 212.
46 Badiou, *Being and Event*: 342.
47 Ibid.: 343.
48 Ibid.: 406.
49 Ibid.: 394.

Chapter 5

1 Badiou, Alain, 'Philosophy, science, mathematics: interview with Alain Badiou', *Collapse: Philosophical Research and Development 1*, (2006): 17.
2 Badiou, *Logics of Worlds: Being and Event, 2*: 75.
3 Badiou, Alain, *The Meaning of Sarkozy*, trans. David Fernbach (London: Verso, 2008): 11.
4 Lacan, Jacques, *The Seminar of Jacques Lacan, Book XX: On Feminine Sexuality, The Limits of Love and Knowledge, 1972–1973*, ed. Jacques-Alain Miller, trans. Bruce Fink (New York: Norton, 1999): 71.
5 Badiou, *Conditions*: 183.
6 Ibid.: 183.
7 Badiou, Alain, 'La scène du deux', *de l'amour*, ed. L'Ecole de la Cause Freudienne (Paris: Flammarion, 1999): 180.
8 Badiou, 'La scène du deux': 183.
9 Badiou, *The Century*: 145.
10 Copjec, Joan, 'Gai savoir sera: the science of love and the insolence of chance', *Alain Badiou: Philosophy and its Conditions*, ed. Gabriel Riera (New York: SUNY Press, 2005): 124.
11 Badiou, *Logics of Worlds: Being and Event, 2*: 384.
12 Badiou, *Being and Event*: 207.
13 Badiou, *Logics of Worlds: Being and Event, 2*: 384.
14 Ibid.: 384.
15 Badiou, *Being and Event*: 175.
16 In *Number and Numbers* Badiou clarifies the ontological regularity of foundation not by turning to some radical event, but rather through recourse to the decidedly mundane example of his own cat, noting that while his cat is an element of the set of living beings whose elements are cells, 'if we decompose a cell into molecules, then into atoms, we eventually reach purely physical elements that don't belong to the set of living beings. There is a certain term (perhaps the cell, in fact) which

belongs to the set of living beings, but none of whose elements belongs to the set of living beings, because those elements all involve only 'inert' physico-chemical materiality. Of this term, which belongs to the set but none of whose elements belong to it, we can say that it grounds the set, or that it is a fundamental term of the set', Badiou, *Number and Numbers*: 71.

17 Picasso, Pablo, *Picasso on Art: A Selection of Views*, ed. Dore Ashton (New York: Viking Press, 1972): 64.
18 Badiou, *Second Manifesto for Philosophy*: 125.
19 Badiou, *Logics of Worlds: Being and Event, 2*: 36, trans. modified.
20 Badiou & Sedofsky, 'Being by numbers': 85.
21 Badiou & Tarby, *Philosophy and the Event*: 71.
22 Badiou, *Logics of Worlds: Being and Event, 2*: 384.
23 Hallward, *Badiou: A Subject to Truth*: 157.
24 Badiou & Sedofsky, 'Being by numbers': 87.
25 Picasso, Pablo, 'Picasso speaks', *Art in Theory 1900–2000: An Anthology of Changing Ideas*, ed. Charles Harrison & Paul Wood (Oxford: Blackwell, 2003): 216.
26 Badiou, *Logics of Worlds: Being and Event, 2*: 71.
27 Badiou, *Ethics: An Essay on the Understanding of Evil*: 12.

Chapter 6

1 Wyatt, Edward, 'In the land of beautiful people, an artist without a face', *The New York Times* (16 September, 2006), http://www.nytimes.com/2006/09/16/arts/design/16bank.html?_r=1&adxnnl=1&adxnnlx=1355239900-9NfINmpLkugBXr9mK94T4w& (accessed 14 July 2016).
2 See www.banksy.co.uk (accessed 14 July 2016).
3 Badiou, *Ethics: An Essay on the Understanding of Evil*: 25.
4 Ibid.: 9.
5 Ibid.: 10.
6 See Derrida, Jacques, *The Gift of Death*, trans. David Wills (Chicago: University of Chicago Press, 1995).
7 Badiou, *Ethics: An Essay on the Understanding of Evil*: 24.
8 Ibid.: 26.
9 Hallward, Peter, 'Translator's introduction', *Ethics: An Essay on the Understanding of Evil*, trans. Peter Hallward (London: Verso, 2001): xiii.
10 Badiou, *Ethics: An Essay on the Understanding of Evil*: 32–3.
11 Ibid.: 16.
12 Ibid.: 12.

13 Lacan, Jacques, *The Seminar of Jacques Lacan, Book VII: The Ethics of Psychoanalysis, 1959–1960*, ed. Jacques-Alain Miller, trans. Dennis Porter (New York: Norton, 1992): 319.
14 Badiou, *Ethics: An Essay on the Understanding of Evil*: 47.
15 Ibid.: 61.
16 Badiou, Alain, and Peter Hallward, 'Beyond formalisation: an interview', *Angelaki: Journal of the Theoretical Humanities* 8/2 (2003): 133.
17 Badiou, *Ethics: An Essay on the Understanding of Evil*: 35.
18 Badiou, Alain, 'On evil: an interview with Alain Badiou,' *Cabinet* 5 (2001), http://www.cabinetmagazine.org/issues/5/alainbadiou.php (accessed 14 July 2016).
19 Badiou, Alain, *Saint Paul: The Foundation of Universalism*, trans. Ray Brassier (Stanford: Stanford University Press, 2003): 92.
20 Badiou, *Conditions*: 234.
21 Badiou, *Ethics: An Essay on the Understanding of Evil*: 79.
22 Badiou & Hallward, 'Beyond formalisation: an interview': 133.
23 Badiou, *Logics of Worlds: Being and Event, 2*: 55.
24 Ibid.: 60.
25 Badiou, *Conditions*: 78.
26 Badiou, *Ethics: An Essay on the Understanding of Evil*: 91.
27 Ibid.: 79.

Conclusion
1 Badiou, *Ethics: An Essay on the Understanding of Evil*: 50.

Bibliography

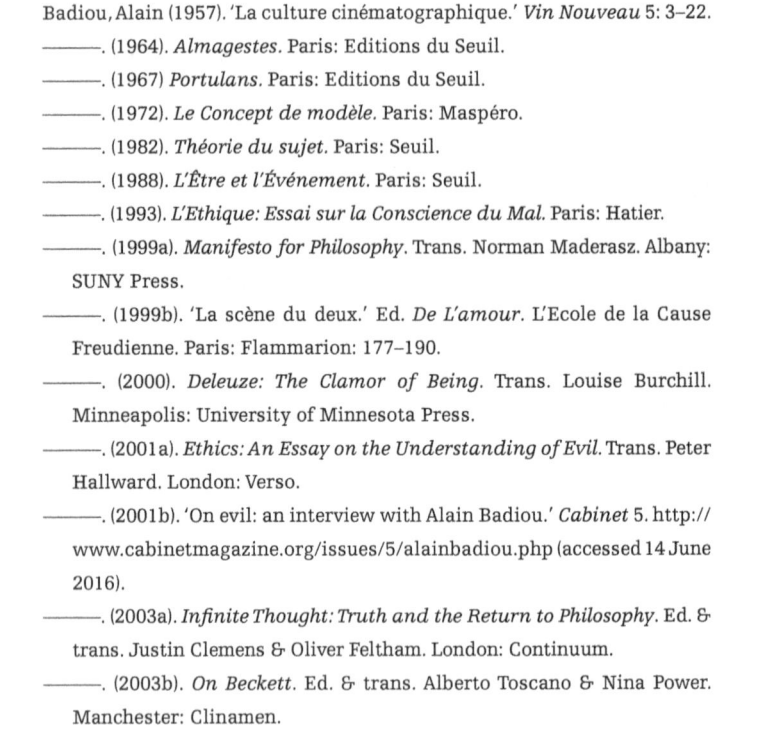

Badiou, Alain (1957). 'La culture cinématographique.' *Vin Nouveau* 5: 3–22.

———. (1964). *Almagestes*. Paris: Editions du Seuil.

———. (1967) *Portulans*. Paris: Editions du Seuil.

———. (1972). *Le Concept de modèle*. Paris: Maspéro.

———. (1982). *Théorie du sujet*. Paris: Seuil.

———. (1988). *L'Être et l'Événement*. Paris: Seuil.

———. (1993). *L'Ethique: Essai sur la Conscience du Mal*. Paris: Hatier.

———. (1999a). *Manifesto for Philosophy*. Trans. Norman Maderasz. Albany: SUNY Press.

———. (1999b). 'La scène du deux.' Ed. *De L'amour*. L'Ecole de la Cause Freudienne. Paris: Flammarion: 177–190.

———. (2000). *Deleuze: The Clamor of Being*. Trans. Louise Burchill. Minneapolis: University of Minnesota Press.

———. (2001a). *Ethics: An Essay on the Understanding of Evil*. Trans. Peter Hallward. London: Verso.

———. (2001b). 'On evil: an interview with Alain Badiou.' *Cabinet* 5. http://www.cabinetmagazine.org/issues/5/alainbadiou.php (accessed 14 June 2016).

———. (2003a). *Infinite Thought: Truth and the Return to Philosophy*. Ed. & trans. Justin Clemens & Oliver Feltham. London: Continuum.

———. (2003b). *On Beckett*. Ed. & trans. Alberto Toscano & Nina Power. Manchester: Clinamen.

———. (2003c). *Saint Paul: The Foundation of Universalism*. Trans. Ray Brassier. Stanford: Stanford University Press.

———. (2004). *Theoretical Writings*. Ed. & trans. Alberto Toscano & Ray Brassier. London: Continuum.

———. (2005a). *Being and Event*. Trans. Oliver Feltham. London: Continuum.

———. (2005b). *Handbook of Inaesthetics*. Trans. Alberto Toscano. Stanford, California: Stanford University Press.

———. (2005c). *Metapolitics*. Trans. Jason Barker. London: Verso.

———. (2006a). *Briefings on Existence: A Short Treatise on Transitory Ontology*. Trans. Norman Maderasz. New York: SUNY.

———. (2006b). 'Drawing.' *Lacanian Ink* 28: 42–9.

———. (2006c). *Logiques des mondes: l'être et l'événement, 2*. Paris: Seuil.

———. (2006d). 'Philosophy, science, mathematics: interview with Alain Badiou.' *Collapse: Philosophical Research and Development* 1: 11–26.

———. (2006e). *Polemics*. Ed. & trans. Steve Corcoran. London: Verso.

———. (2007a). *The Century*. Trans. Alberto Toscano. Cambridge: Polity.

———. (2007b). *The Concept of Model*. Trans. Zachery Luke Fraser & Tzuchien Tho. Melbourne: re.press.

———. (2007c). *De quoi Sarkozy est-il le nom?* Paris: Nouvelle Éditions Lignes.

———. (2007d). 'Towards a new concept of existence.' *Lacanian Ink* 29: 63–72.

———. (2008a). *Conditions*. Trans. Stephen Corcoran. London: Continuum.

———. (2008b). *The Meaning of Sarkozy*. Trans. David Fernbach. London: Verso.

———. (2008c). *Number and Numbers*. Trans. Robin Mackay. London: Polity.

———. (2008d). 'Rhapsody for the theatre: a short philosophical treatise.' *Theatre Survey* 49/2: 187–238.

———. (2008e). 'Some remarks concerning Marcel Duchamp'. *The Symptom* 9. http://www.lacan.com/symptom9_articles/badiou29.html (accessed 14 July 2016).

———. (2009a). *Logics of Worlds: Being and Event, 2*. Trans. Alberto Toscano. London: Continuum.

———. (2009b). *Theory of the Subject*. Trans. Bruno Bosteels. London: Continuum.

———. (2010a). *Le Fini et l'Infini*. Paris: Bayard Centurion.

———. (2010b). *Five Lessons on Wagner*. Trans. Susan Spitzer. New York: Verso.

———. (2011). *Second Manifesto for Philosophy*. Trans. Louise Burchill. Cambridge: Polity.

———. (2013). *Cinema*. Ed. Antoine de Baecque. Trans. Susan Spitzer. Cambridge: Polity Press.

———. (2014). *Mathematics of the Transcendental*. Ed. & trans. A.J. Bartlett & Alex Ling. London: Bloomsbury.

Badiou, Alain, and Bruno Bosteels (2005). 'Can Change Be Thought: A Dialogue with Alain Badiou.' *Alain Badiou: Philosophy and its Conditions*. Ed. Gabriel Riera. New York: SUNY Press: 237–61.

Badiou, Alain, and Elie During (2005). 'Le 21e siècle n'a pas commencé: entretien avec Elie During.' *Art Press* 310: 56–8.

Badiou, Alain and Marcel Gauchet (2016). *What Is To Be Done?: A Dialogue on Communism, Capitalism, and the Future of Democracy*. Trans. Susan Spitzer. Cambridge: Polity Press.

Badiou, Alain, and Peter Hallward (2003). 'Beyond formalisation: an interview.' *Angelaki: Journal of the Theoretical Humanities* 8/2: 111–36.

Badiou, Alain, and Lauren Sedofsky (1994). 'Being by numbers.' *Artforum* 33/2: 84–7/118/123–4.

———. (2006). 'Matters of appearance: an interview with Alain Badiou.' *Artforum* 45/3: 246–253/322.

Badiou, Alain, and Fabien Tarby (2013). *Philosophy and the Event*. Trans. Louise Burchill. Cambridge: Polity Press.

Bartlett, A. J. (2011). *Badiou and Plato: An Education by Truths*. Edinburgh: Edinburgh University Press.

Bazin, André (1967). *What is Cinema?: Volume 1*. Ed. & trans. Hugh Gray. Berkeley, California: University of California Press.

———. (1971). *What is Cinema?: Volume 2*. Ed. & trans. Hugh Gray. Berkeley, California: University of California Press.

Beckett, Samuel (1990). *Samuel Beckett: The Complete Dramatic Works*. London: Faber and Faber.

Copjec, Joan (2005). 'Gai savoir sera: the science of love and the insolence of chance.' *Alain Badiou: Philosophy and its Conditions*. Ed. Gabriel Riera. New York: SUNY Press: 119–135.

Critchley, Simon (2007). 'To be or not to be is not the question: on Beckett's *Film*.' *Film-Philosophy*, 11/2: 108–121.

De Duve, Thierry (1991). *Pictorial Nominalism: On Marcel Duchamp's Passage from Painting to the Readymade*. Trans. Dana Polen. Minneapolis: University of Minnesota Press.

———. (1996). *Kant After Duchamp*. Cambridge, Massachusetts: MIT Press.

Deleuze, Gilles (1997). *Essays Critical and Clinical*. Trans. Daniel W. Smith & Michael A. Greco. Minneapolis: University of Minnesota Press.

———. (2005). *Cinema 1: The Movement-Image*. Trans. Hugh Tomlinson & Barbara Habberjam. London: Continuum.

Derrida, Jacques (1995). *The Gift of Death*. Trans. David Wills. Chicago: University of Chicago Press.

Dolar, Mladen (1992). 'Hitchcock's objects.' *Everything You Always Wanted to Know About Lacan (But Were Afraid to Ask Hitchcock)*. Ed. Slavoj Žižek. London: Verso: 31–46.

Duchamp, Marcel (1989a). *Notes*. Ed. Paul Matisse. Boston: G. K. Hall.

———. (1989b). *The Writings of Marcel Duchamp*. Eds. Michel Sanouillet & Elmer Peterson. New York: De Capo Press.

Feshbach, Sidney (1999). 'Unswamping a backwater: on Samuel Beckett's *Film*.' *Samuel Beckett and the Arts: Music, Visual Arts, and Non-Print Media*. Ed. Lois Oppenheim. New York: Garland Publishing: 333–363.

Formis, Barbara (2004). 'Event and ready-made: delayed sabotage.' *Communication & Cognition* 27/3: 247–261.

Greenberg, Clement (2003). 'Modernist painting.' *Art in Theory 1900–2000: An Anthology of Changing Ideas*. Eds. Charles Harrison & Paul Wood. Oxford: Blackwell: 773–9.

Hallward, Peter (2001). 'Translator's introduction.' *Ethics: An Essay on the Understanding of Evil*. Trans. Peter Hallward. London: Verso: ivii–xlvii.

———. (2003). *Badiou: A Subject to Truth*. London: University of Minnesota Press.

Hausdorff, Felix (1962). *Set Theory*. New York: Chelsea Publications.

Lacan, Jacques (1991). *The Seminar of Jacques Lacan, Book I: Freud's Papers on Technique 1953–1954*. Ed. Jacques-Alain Miller. Trans. John Forrester. New York: Norton.

———. (1992). *The Seminar of Jacques Lacan, Book VII: The Ethics of Psychoanalysis, 1959–1960*. Ed. Jacques-Alain Miller. Trans. Dennis Porter. New York: Norton.

———. (1999). *The Seminar of Jacques Lacan, Book XX: On Feminine Sexuality, The Limits of Love and Knowledge, 1972–1973*. Ed. Jacques-Alain Miller. Trans. Bruce Fink. New York: Norton.

Ling, Alex (2011). *Badiou and Cinema*. Edinburgh: Edinburgh University Press.

Mallarmé, Stéphane (1994). *Collected Poems*. Trans. Henry Weinfield. Berkeley: University of California Press.

Malevich, Kasimir (2003). 'From cubism to futurism to suprematism: the new realism in painting.' *Art in Theory 1900–2000: An Anthology of Changing Ideas*. Eds. Charles Harrison & Paul Wood. Oxford: Blackwell: 173–83.

Norton, Louise (1917). 'Buddah of the bathroom.' *The Blind Man* 2: 5–6.

Picasso, Pablo (1972). *Picasso on Art: A Selection of Views*. Ed. Dore Ashton. New York: Viking Press.

———. (2003). 'Picasso speaks.' *Art in Theory 1900–2000: An Anthology of Changing Ideas*. Eds. Charles Harrison & Paul Wood. Oxford: Blackwell: 215–7.

Potts, Alex (2000). *The Sculptural Imagination: Figurative, Modernist, Minimalist*. New Haven: Yale University Press.

Schneider, Alan (1972). 'On directing film.' *Film by Samuel Beckett*. London: Faber and Faber: 63–94.

Tomkins, Calvin (2013). *Marcel Duchamp: The Afternoon Interviews*. Brooklyn: Badlands Unlimited.

Unattributed (1917). 'The Richard Mutt Case.' *The Blind Man* 2: 3–4.

Wyatt, Edward (2006). 'In the land of beautiful people, an artist without a face.' *The New York Times* (16 September). http://www.nytimes.com/2006/09/16/arts/design/16bank.html?_r=1&adxnnl=1&adxnnlx=1355239900-9NfINmpLkugBXr9mK94T4w& (accessed 13 June 2016).

Index

Althusser, Louis 114
antiphilosophy 63, 147
appearing 13, 35–6, 38–42, 46–7, 49, 53, 55–6, 58–63, 71–3, 81–2, 95, 98, 114–19, 135, 151, 160
Aristotle 22
axiom (set theory) 23, 33–5, 71, 87–90, 116, 119, 129, 160

Banksy 136–41
Bazin, André 46–7
Beckett, Samuel 53–62, 122, 142, 154
being 22–9, 31–3, 35–6, 38–42, 46–8, 54–6, 58–9, 61–3, 71–2, 75, 77, 81, 83, 86, 89, 90–1, 97, 104, 106–7, 114–19, 131–2, 135, 160
being-there 36, 42, 47, 116, 119
belonging (set theory) 3, 34–5, 39–40, 71, 87, 107–8, 129, 132, 165, 167–8
See also presentation
Benjamin, Walter 46
Berkeley, Bishop 54, 60–1
betrayal 149–50, 152–4
body (subject) 16, 60, 98–100, 103–7, 109, 117, 119–20, 132, 134, 145, 150, 151
Braque, Georges 130

Cantor, Georg 23, 36, 90–1, 106, 118–19, 156
category theory 36, 40, 90, 116, 118, 135
cogito 55, 57–8, 60–2, 114

Cohen, Paul J. 90–1, 107–8
conditions of philosophy 3–4, 8–9, 32, 43–5, 77–9, 90–2, 113, 118, 140, 148, 157
count-as-one 25–8, 31, 34–5, 40, 71, 87–8, 98, 129, 163

death 42, 73, 148
decision 16, 21, 25, 50, 70, 88, 94, 99, 100, 126, 154, 157
See also point
Deleuze, Gilles 61–3, 114, 154
Derrida, Jacques 143, 145
Descartes, René 56
Duchamp, Marcel 3, 67–8, 73–7, 80–5, 101–4, 164

empty set 35, 40, 87
See also void
ethics 113–15, 141–50, 152–4, 156
event 1, 6–8, 10–11, 13–18, 21, 34, 55, 68–77, 80–106, 109, 114–22, 124–9, 132–6, 138–41, 145–6, 148–54, 156–7, 163–4, 166
evil 142–3, 147–54
existence 10, 14–16, 18, 32, 42, 53, 71–73, 77, 102, 116, 156

faithful subject 8, 10, 16, 97–9, 106–7, 117, 136, 154, 148–51, 153
See also fidelity
fidelity 10, 97, 128, 133, 145–6, 148–9, 152–3

Fleming, Victor 13
forcing 90, 108–9, 117, 133, 139, 150, 153–4
Foucault, Michel 4, 114
Freud, Sigmund 114

generic 8, 11–12, 17, 43, 54, 56, 58, 61, 63, 73, 78–80, 86, 90, 97, 104, 106–9, 113–15, 117–18, 120, 128, 130–2, 138, 140, 157, 166
See also conditions of philosophy; set theory; truth-procedure
Giacometti, Alberto 121
Godard, Jean-Luc 45, 48
Gödel, Kurt 90
good 142–4, 146–50, 152–4
Greenberg, Clement 29, 80, 159

Hitchcock, Alfred 51
Husserl, Edmund 52, 56

immortality 99, 106, 134, 142, 152, 154
inaesthetics 44, 77–82, 84, 101, 118
inclusion (set theory) 87, 97–8, 107, 139, 165
See also representation
indiscernibility 31–2, 70, 77, 83–5, 106–9, 130, 132–3, 146, 154–5
inexistence 10, 14–16, 32, 42, 72–3, 77, 82, 98, 102, 116, 140
infinite 12, 15, 23, 38, 80, 81, 88, 95, 97–9, 101, 103–9, 114, 117–19, 128, 133–4, 155–6
intervention 99, 113

Kant, Immanuel 142
knowledge 6, 9–12, 25, 43, 70, 81, 85, 88–9, 102, 106, 108–9, 117–18, 121, 126, 139, 146–7, 153, 155, 157

Lacan, Jacques 6, 12, 25, 114, 120, 146–7
Levinas, Emmanuel 61, 114–15, 143, 145

logic 7, 14, 32, 36, 38–42, 46–8, 53, 63, 68, 72–3, 86, 90, 114, 116–17, 131–2, 135–6, 160–1
See also category theory; onto-logy; phenomenology
love 3, 7, 9, 43–4, 78, 115, 118, 120–3, 125–8, 148–9
See also conditions of philosophy

Malevich, Kasimir 3, 29–32, 36–9, 80, 83, 85
Mallarmé, Stéphane 38, 91–6, 101, 154
Marxism 15–18
materialist dialectic 7, 89, 91, 109, 157
mathematics 2–3, 5, 7, 11–12, 21–3, 32–6, 45, 69–70, 87, 89–91, 106–8, 114–19, 135, 156, 157, 160–1
See also Cantor, Georg; generic; ontology; set theory
Merleau-Ponty, Maurice 114
metastructure 27, 88
modernism 29, 79, 85, 159–60
multiplicity 1, 3, 5, 13, 22–8, 31–6, 38–42, 48–9, 71–2, 90, 94–8, 101, 107–9, 114, 116, 120, 129, 135, 140, 144, 147, 160, 163, 165–6

Nietzsche, Friedrich 99

objects (theory of) 22–4, 39–42, 47, 50–3, 58, 60–3, 71–3, 97–100, 116–17, 135, 146, 150
ontology 2, 7, 21–5, 27–9, 32–6, 40, 42–4, 69, 71–2, 88, 90–1, 97, 102, 115–18, 135, 138, 156–7, 160
See also mathematics; onto-logy; set theory
onto-logy 36, 47–8, 53, 62–3, 69, 116, 132, 135, 160–1
See also category theory; logic; mathematics; ontology; phenomenology; set theory

organ 100, 109, 114
See also body; point

Parmenides 23
phenomenology 7, 39, 43, 52–3, 56, 71–2, 77, 98, 114, 116, 131, 135
See also logic; onto-logy
Picasso 25, 73, 130–1, 134
Plato 2, 23–4, 148
point 16, 99–100, 103, 149, 155
politics 7, 13–18, 25, 27, 43–4, 120, 139–40, 142, 149, 156, 163
See also conditions of philosophy
presentation 15, 24–9, 31–2, 34–5, 38, 46, 77, 88, 94, 95, 98, 103, 116, 120, 163, 165

representation 14–15, 27–8, 72, 86, 87–8, 98, 107, 120, 129, 138, 165
Resnais, Alain 122, 124, 126–7
Robert, Hubert 49
Rothko, Mark 36–9

Schneider, Alan 53, 59
Schönberg, Arnold 105
science 9, 22, 24, 42–4, 78, 91, 115, 118–19, 128, 135
See also conditions of philosophy
set theory 23, 33–6, 90, 107, 115–16, 118–19, 135, 157, 160
See also mathematics; ontology
simulacrum 149, 152–3
site 8, 10, 13–14, 16, 18, 70–5, 81, 91, 102, 129–30, 140, 163–4
See also event
state (of the situation) 7–10, 13–18, 21, 26–7, 34, 69–70, 72, 74–6, 81, 86–9, 91, 97, 103, 106–7, 109, 116, 120, 126, 136, 138–40, 143–4, 163, 165
subtraction 9–11, 23–5, 27–32, 36–8, 46, 48–9, 56, 58, 62–3, 81, 85–6, 91, 105, 108, 115, 117, 126, 148, 153, 166

terror 89, 145–53
time 12, 55, 123–5, 132–4, 157
trace 8, 10, 16, 69, 73, 82, 94, 96–7, 98–100, 104–6, 109, 117, 119–20, 122, 134, 150–1, 154, 166
transcendental 39–42, 49–52, 71, 73, 103, 116, 135
truth-procedure 8–11, 13, 16, 18, 45, 99, 102, 104–6, 113, 118, 127–8, 130, 138–9, 143, 155–7

undecidable 25, 70, 84, 94–6, 108, 125–6
universal 5, 9, 12, 17–18, 22, 69, 72, 78–9, 89, 97, 107, 117, 122, 128, 130–2, 134, 136, 142, 149, 157

void 1, 10, 13–15, 23, 26–31, 34–5, 37–8, 40, 52, 56, 61, 63, 72, 74, 77, 87–9, 93–6, 98, 102, 109, 116, 120, 122, 127, 129–30, 132, 138, 140, 144–5, 149–52, 160, 165

world 5, 7, 10–12, 14–15, 36, 38–42, 49–53, 60, 68, 70–1, 73–6, 80, 83–6, 89–90, 97–100, 102, 105–6, 108–9, 116–17, 119–20, 128, 130–2, 135–6, 138, 140, 151–2, 155, 158

drawing on a roller blind — black.

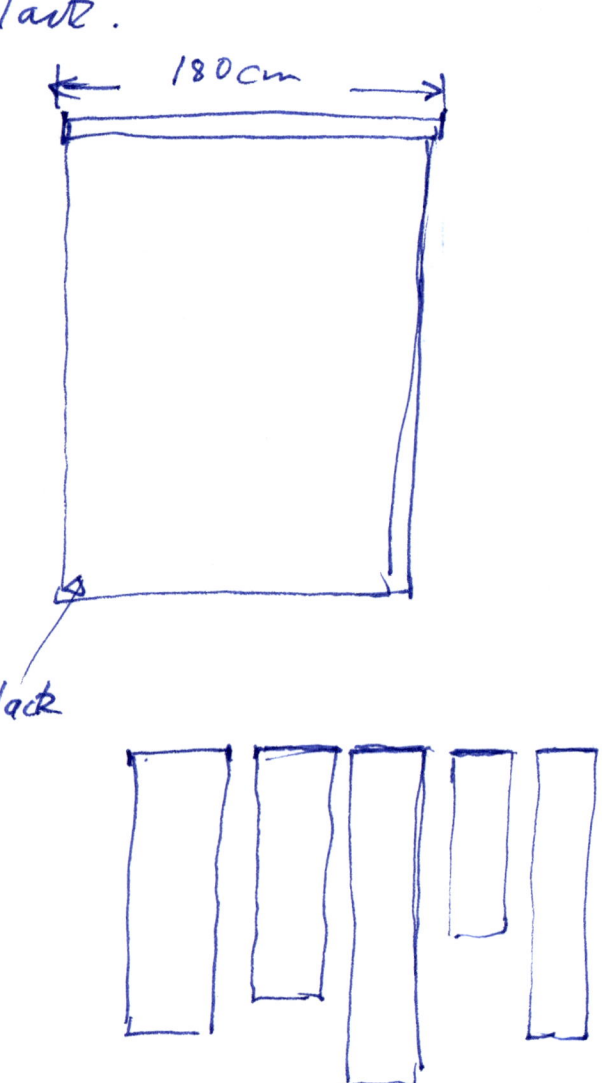

180cm

black

chord:

content / sound
Drawings, videos

Things to do —
- order roller blind + velcro
- Lectern —
- video
- check 21'-31' screens
- active speaker-deck
- loudspeaker stands
- iPad anti-reflection film

Main

active speaker.

To buy

Black roller blinds, 21' screen
active speaker

drawings

21' screen

iPad

hematite coated...
backgrnd to ~~the~~ drawings

Two speaker installatn.

Lectern & teleprompter

drawings of sound.
case.

HDMI Mains

small metal/Al box

[MP] [AS]

Mains

HDMI

[MP] [AS] [Amp]

Box viewer — text?